STAINED GLASS

STEP-BY-STEP CRAFTS

STAINED GLASS

LYNETTE WRIGLEY

CREATIVE
PUBLISHING
international

MINNETONKA, MINNESOTA

First published in the USA and Canada by
Creative Publishing international, Inc.

CREATIVE
PUBLISHING
international

5900 Green Oak Drive
Minnetonka, MN 55343
1-800-328-3895

ISBN 0-86573-347-3

Photographer: Colin Bowling
Project Editor: Alice Bell
Editor: Anke Ueberg

Editorial Direction: Rosemary Wilkinson

10 9 8 7 6 5 4 3 2 1

Reproduction by PICA Colour Separation,
Singapore
Printed and bound in Malaysia by
Times Offset (M) Sdn. Bhd.

Contributors

Anna Sklovsky
26 Stockwell Park Crescent
London SW9 0DE
Tel: 020 7733 4500
Fax: 020 7737 4619

Anna Sklovsky also teaches at
The Mary Ward Centre
42 Queen Square
London WC1N 3AQ

Anji Marfleet
Through the Looking Glass
12 Aspen Court
Emley nr. Huddersfield
West Yorks HD8 9RW
Tel/Fax: 01924 840315

Annette Reed
12 Cashmere Close
Shenley Brook End
Milton Keynes MK5 7FA
Tel: 01908 507517

Janice Issitt
E-mail: kenissitt@net.ntl.com
Tel: 020 8341 7947

Redford Studios Employment
   and Training Project
Hillingdon Mind
   Enterprises Ltd.
Aston House, Redford Way
Uxbridge, Middx UB8 1SZ
Tel: 01895 254379
Fax: 01895 811355

Acknowledgments

Thank you to Anji Marfleet, Annette Reed and Anna Sklovsky for
the loan of their transparencies and for allowing us to show their
beautiful work. Also a big thanks to Janice Issitt for her help and
time in contributing her delightful flower designs for photography
and publication. Many thanks also to all at the Redford Studio
Employment and Training Project at Hillingdon Mind for
allowing me to pick from their treasure trove of imaginative items
for the gallery on page 74. Last but not least, a thank you to Marc
Gerstein of Lead & Light for the loan of all tools and equipment.

The photograph on page 15 shows a picture of powder-blue
surgeonfish, which is credited to Linda Pitkin.

Contents

Introduction

More than ever before people are discovering the rich and versatile craft of stained glass as an expression of creativity. Whether it's individuals seeking a hobby, or professional artists turning to a new medium, working with stained glass is a challenging and rewarding pursuit.

Stained glass is available in the most wonderful diversity of colors and textures, and is often something to behold in its own right even before being turned into a piece of work. Projects in the book demonstrate how to take advantage of this unique material, and to think of glass not only as transmitting light, but to consider other ideas where its decorative quality can be exhibited.

The aim of this book is to provide beginners with information and helpful ideas for making items for the home. It includes fifteen step-by-step projects designed for beginners and those with only a little experience to achieve striking results. Selected to show a variety of decorative glass work, the projects range from small three-dimensional items to colorful mirror frames and windows including a leaded light and an appliqué panel.

Read the "Getting Started" section before beginning the projects so as to familiarize yourself with the methods you will encounter later, from how to cut glass to soldering, copper foiling and leading. There is also a list of the few specialist tools and materials required for this surprisingly accessible craft.

Most of the projects use the basic techniques of cutting glass, copper foiling and soldering, which can be mastered with practice and a little patience. There are also examples of decorative effects using etching cream and glass appliqué. Although colors and types of glass are suggested for each project, the choice is ultimately your own. Even clear glass has a lot to offer. The size of the glass required is usually an approximation: it is always advisable to buy more than you think you will need.

As you progress through the projects, you will gain confidence in applying and mastering new skills. Your creativity will be challenged, and you may want to proceed to design and execute your own ideas. However tempting though, keep your ideas simple when venturing into your own designs for the first time. It is a boring fact that there is nothing more off-putting than taking on a challenge that you cannot sustain. So, do resist making that Tiffany lampshade requiring six hundred and thirty-five pieces of glass until later.

In the Window Gallery on page 74, you will find examples of the work of contemporary stained glass artists today. Although some of these pieces may demonstrate techniques outside the range of this book, the idea is to inspire you and illustrate the fascinating potential of stained glass. My hope is that these examples will also serve to encourage you to pursue and explore the compelling and creative challenge of this craft still further.

Getting Started

There are surprisingly few special tools required to start working with stained glass as a beginner to the subject. However, these few tools are essential and worth investing in because they will make the whole process of learning this craft easier and more enjoyable. At the back of the book you will find a list of suppliers who offer a mail order service, but you can also check the telephone directory for outlets in your area.

Familiarize yourself with the tools and equipment and how to use them. Wire and jewelry pliers have been used in some projects. Many types of wire are available in local hardware shops, and the jewelry pliers and silver-coated wire can be bought from craft suppliers.

Read through the check list of safety notes very thoroughly.

When working with glass, use common sense and handle it carefully. Small nicks and cuts are inevitable from time to time, but you should rarely experience anything worse. Keep a first aid box and a box of bandages handy just in case.

GLASS

A specialist stained glass supplier is the best source of materials and information about the many types of colored glass that are produced. Most suppliers also offer a mail order service. However, until you are familiar with the wide range of colored glass that is available try to visit a stockist first to see the varieties on sale.

Glass can be divided into two main categories: antique glass and rolled glass, better known as cathedral glass.

Antique glass

Antique glass is blown by mouth as opposed to being machine-made. The name does not refer to the age of the glass but to the centuries-old technique by which it is made. Each sheet of antique glass is unique, having its own particular qualities, irregularities and range of colors.

Rolled or cathedral glass

This name refers to glass which is made by machine rather than by hand. There are many types of machine-made glass made

SAFETY CHECKLIST

Always keep glass and chemicals in a safe place when not in use, out of the reach of children and animals.

Always wear protective glasses when cutting, filing or grinding glass.

Wear rubber or protective gloves when working with chemicals such as patina and etching paste.

Always have a dustpan and brush handy and frequently brush away the small slivers and shards of glass that will accumulate on the work surface. NEVER use your bare hands to sweep away pieces of glass.

Dispose of glass carefully. If it goes into a dustbin, put it into thick cardboard boxes first.

Keep your work area tidy.

Never attempt to catch a piece of falling glass.

Hold the soldering iron by the handle only.

Work in a well-ventilated area when soldering.

Use a metal stand to rest the soldering iron on when in use and switch it off when it is not.

Keep some bandages and a first aid kit handy.

Always wash your hands before eating after handling lead, solder or any chemicals.

Red water

Streaky

Opalescent

Clear textured

Roundel

Blue water

Amber water

by different companies, and each may have different cutting properties and characteristics. Listed below are just a few of the many types you will come across.

• **Opalescent glass**
Most but not all opalescent glass is machine-made. It is characterized by its opacity, in contrast to the other types of machine-made glass which are transparent. It is seldom one color; rather it may be a mixture of whirling colors or streaks spreading through the sheet. It comes in various degrees of opacity.

• **Streaky glass**
Two or more colors are swirled together in one piece of glass.

• **Water glass**
Water glass is a trade name rather than a specific type of glass and is made by the Spectrum Glass Company. This glass has an even, wavy appearance on the surface and is available in a beautiful range of vibrant colors.

• **Semi-antique glass**
This glass has a distinct surface pattern of tiny striations, intended to simulate the appearance of mouth-blown glass but without the variation. It is available in many colors and easy to cut, making it ideal for beginners.

• **Iridized glass**
This type of glass has a surface appearance similar to oil on water and is available in most kinds of rolled glass.

edge. They can be foiled or leaded and included in lamps, window panels and three-dimensional projects.

Bevels
These are clear shapes of glass with smooth polished bevelled edges. Available in a variety of shapes and sizes, they may be foiled or leaded and incorporated into window panels. See page 42 for a delicate design using clear bevels and glass.

GLASS ACCESSORIES

Nuggets
These are thick, rounded pieces of colored or clear glass with a flattened side, available in various sizes. Nuggets can be foiled (see right) and incorporated into panels, windows and lamps.

Roundels
These are round machine-pressed or hand-spun pieces of glass with a smooth

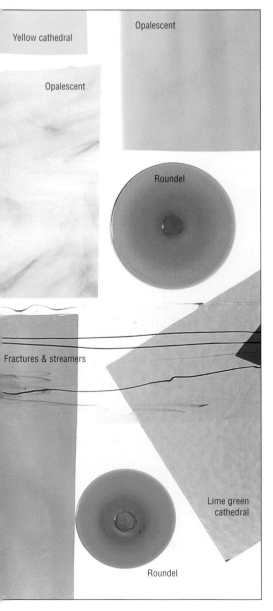

Yellow cathedral

Opalescent

Opalescent

Roundel

Fractures & streamers

Lime green cathedral

Roundel

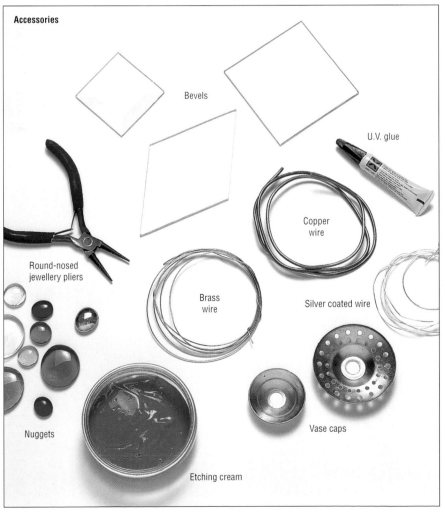

Accessories

Bevels

U.V. glue

Round-nosed jewellery pliers

Copper wire

Brass wire

Silver coated wire

Nuggets

Vase caps

Etching cream

TOOLS AND EQUIPMENT

Glass cutters
The most important skill to learn when working with glass is how to cut it. There are several varieties of glass cutters on the market and new ones are continually being developed. Avoid the cheap cutters you may find in a local hardware store and invest in a good quality cutter from a stained glass supplier.

• Carbide steel wheel cutter
This cutter usually has a ball shape fashioned onto the end of the handle which is used for tapping the scored glass. Some have a replaceable cutting wheel. To prolong the wheel's life, keep a jar with a cotton pad soaked in cutting oil and occasionally dip the wheel into it.

• Tungsten carbide wheel cutter
This type of cutter usually has a built-in oil reservoir in the handle. It is more expensive than the steel wheel cutter but it has a longer handle which most people find more comfortable to use, especially those new to the craft.

• Pistol grip cutter
This is the same type of tool as the tungsten carbide wheel cutter, but with a differently shaped handle.

Cutting oil
This is useful for prolonging the life of the glass cutter (see Carbide steel wheel cutter) and improving your score.

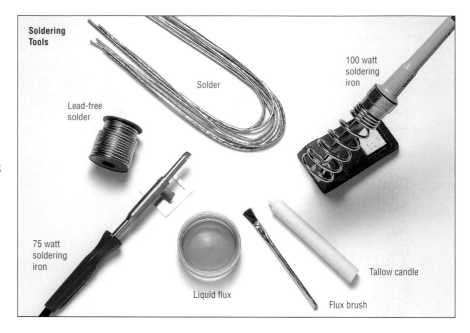

Soldering Tools
Lead-free solder
Solder
100 watt soldering iron
75 watt soldering iron
Liquid flux
Tallow candle
Flux brush

Cutting square
The lip on the lower edge of this cutting square helps when squaring off glass at a perfect right angle. Use the long side of the square with the glass cutter for scoring straight lines.

Pliers
• Grozer/breaker pliers
Pliers for glass work should not be confused with ordinary household pliers. Specifically designed for working with glass, grozer/breaker pliers or combination pliers have curved jaws for gripping glass and can be used both for breaking glass and for nipping off small irregular points from the edges of glass. The insides of the jaws are serrated and can be used to groze off slivers of glass remaining on the edges after breaking.

• Running pliers
These plastic or metal pliers are designed for breaking long, narrow sections of glass.

Carborundum stone
Sharp edges can be removed by rubbing the glass edges on this stone prior to copper foiling (see page 48, step 4).

Electric glass grinder
You may wish to invest in this piece of equipment once you have some experience of glass work. This machine has a water-cooled grinding head which will not only rapidly blunt the sharp edges of the glass but can also be used to grind away sections of glass.

Soldering iron
Soldering is the process of joining two metals together and is necessary for both copper foil and lead work. You will need a soldering iron specifically designed for stained glass work, with a minimum of 75 watts. Small soldering irons used for electrical repairs will not be suitable. Always acquire a stand for the iron when making your purchase.

Solder
Solder is a mixture of tin and lead and is available in lengths or by the roll. Solder with a higher tin content will have a lower melting point and will flow quicker, with a more silvery finish. The combination can be 50/50 tin/lead or 60/40 tin/lead. Lead-free solder is also available in 500 g (1 1b) rolls. You may wish to use this for making jewelry.

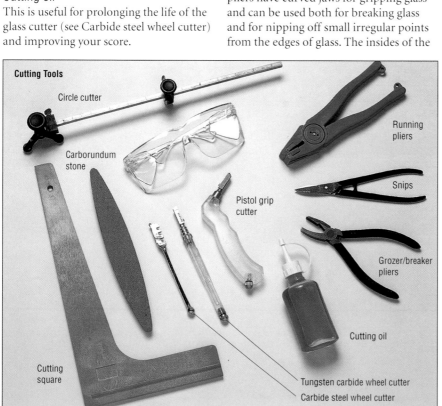

Cutting Tools
Circle cutter
Carborundum stone
Running pliers
Snips
Pistol grip cutter
Grozer/breaker pliers
Cutting oil
Cutting square
Tungsten carbide wheel cutter
Carbide steel wheel cutter

Flux

Flux is applied before joining two metals together, allowing the solder to flow easily when melted with the soldering iron. Flux is available as a liquid or paste for copper foiled work, or as a solid substance called "tallow candle" for lead work.

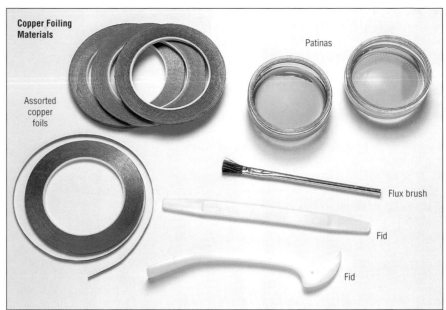

Copper Foiling Materials

Assorted copper foils

Patinas

Flux brush

Fid

Fid

Tip cleaner

As you work, black deposits will accumulate on the tip of the soldering iron. While you can clean the tip from time to time by wiping it on the sponge of the iron rest (see above), there is also a chemical tip cleaner that will remove the deposits and enable the iron to transfer heat more efficiently.

Copper foil

Copper foil is a thin copper "tape" with an adhesive backing. It is wrapped around the glass prior to soldering. It comes in a variety of widths; their suitability will depend on the thickness and size of the piece of glass. Where two pieces of copper foiled glass are placed together and soldered, the resulting seam of solder will be wider or narrower depending on the width of the copper foil. Extremely versatile and suitable for both small and large window panels, it is especially useful for three-dimensional items.

Patina

Patina is a liquid that can be applied to the solder of a finished project to turn the silver-colored solder either a grey/black or copper color. Rubber gloves must be worn when applying patina, and the project must be washed well in warm soapy water and rinsed thoroughly with clear water afterward.

Fid (Lathekin)

This unattractively named implement is amazingly useful. It can be used to press and smooth down the copper foil onto the sides and edges of the glass. The fids with a claw shape on one end are also used for opening crushed channels of lead cames.

Lead cames

Lead cames come in lengths of 6 feet (1.85 m) and in a variety of widths and profiles. They have an empty channel along each side for holding the glass. For the leaded panel on page 58, a ¼" (6 mm) round lead came was used for the internal leading and a ½" (12 mm) flat lead came for the perimeter.

Lead vice

It is essential to straighten out any bends and kinks in a piece of lead before use. The lead vice should be fixed to a sturdy table or workbench and one end of the lead clamped into the vice. The other end of the length of lead should be held with pliers and tugged gently to stretch and straighten it. Alternatively, two people can stretch a piece of lead by holding one end each with a set of pliers. Be cautious though: if you pull too hard on the lead you may find yourself flying backwards if the lead snaps. Short, gentle tugs are sufficient.

Lead knife

This knife has a curved blade which cuts through lead cames. The heavy handle is useful for tapping in horseshoe nails.

Horseshoe nails

These flat-sided nails are used to hold lead and glass in place while working on a leaded light prior to soldering (see page 62).

Lead light cement

This is a specialist putty for weather-proofing and strengthening a leaded light or panel. The oily putty is brushed into the channels, filling the gap between the glass and the lead. Whiting, a chalk-like powder, is sprinkled over the panel afterward to help dry the cement and clean the glass, then brushed off.

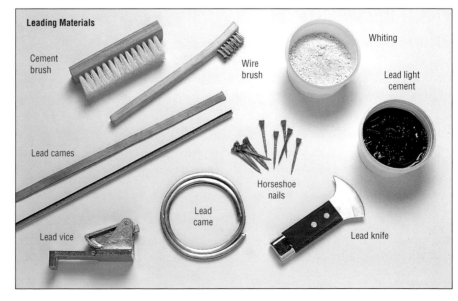

Leading Materials

Cement brush

Wire brush

Whiting

Lead light cement

Lead cames

Horseshoe nails

Lead vice

Lead came

Lead knife

Etching cream

Etching cream will produce a lightly frosted effect on a glass surface. It is a useful alternative to sandblasting or acid etching and gives a similar but softer finish. It should be used with caution: always wear rubber gloves and follow the manufacturer's instructions.

Glass bonding adhesive (U.V. glue)

This adhesive cures in sunlight and forms a strong, clear bond. It is used in the appliqué project (page 76) and also for attaching the eyes and fins on the tropical fish panel (see page 73). It is available from stained glass suppliers but can also be found in hardware shops.

CUTTING GLASS

Holding the cutter

Holding the glass cutter may initially feel uncomfortable or strange, but there are several different ways of holding it and they all enable you to produce a score on the glass. However, the aim is to score the glass following a design or a pattern and also to exert enough pressure with the cutter to achieve a successful score. The picture below shows one possible method which may be the most comfortable,

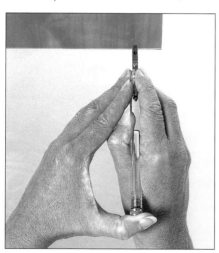

especially for beginners. Some people may find it sufficient to use only one hand to hold the cutter and to exert the required pressure, but placing the thumb of your free hand on top of the handle and the fingers down the side (see above) to steady the cutter can make all the difference.

Practise on clear glass first. Begin by making random scores to start with, then try following the lines of a pattern placed

beneath the glass. Keep the work close to you and work on a table that is not higher than waist level. Don't crouch over the glass while you score but stand fairly upright. The pressure you exert on the cutter should come from the shoulder.

It is best to push the cutter forward, enabling you to follow the line of your design accurately. Tilt the cutter toward you from a 90° angle, just enough to see the wheel, press down and push it along the line of the pattern. You can start the score just inside the edge of the glass and release the pressure $\frac{1}{16}$" (1 mm) before you reach the other edge.

The score

The wheel of the glass cutter will create a line – the score – on the surface of the glass. The score creates a fracture, enabling you to break the glass apart. Never stop the score in the middle of a piece of glass: you must always take the score from one edge of the glass to the other or stop only when you reach another score that you have already made. You should be able to see and "hear" the score being made. Do not go over a score a second time. It will not improve the score and will ruin the cutter. Always score the glass on the smoother side if you are using glass with a "texture" on one side.

Breaking the score

The score can be broken in various ways. Which method you use depends on the

size and type of the glass, whether it is easy to break and whether the score is straight or curved.

You can use your hands by grasping the glass close to either side of the score line. Curl the fingers underneath as shown below and grip the glass. A sharp outward twist of the wrists will snap the glass apart. You can also grip the glass with one hand and use the pliers with the other. This is especially useful if one section of the scored glass is a narrow strip. Always grip the glass very close to the score.

Some types of glass break more easily than others. To encourage an obstinate score to break, you can tap the glass using the ball end of the cutter. Hold the glass with one hand and "tap" immediately beneath the scored line. You can see how the score changes in appearance as it fractures. Tapping is sometimes essential when trying to break a curved score.

Scoring straight lines

Use the cutting square to score straight lines. Practice first on scrap glass. Place the cutting square on the glass and press it down very firmly with one hand. Hold the cutter at the top of the square and press it down, drawing it toward you. It is important to keep the square steady and at the same time apply pressure on the cutter as you pull it down the side of the square.

The picture below shows the position of the cutting square for scoring a straight line. There is a space – the shoulder – on either side of the wheel of the cutter. Before starting a score, position the wheel of the cutter on the line you want, then bring the cutting square alongside it, parallel with the line. Once the cutting square has been placed in the correct position, apply pressure with one hand to hold it in place and use the other to begin scoring the glass.

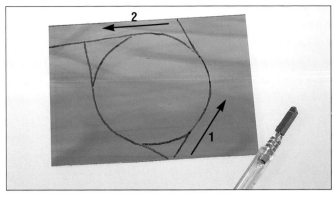
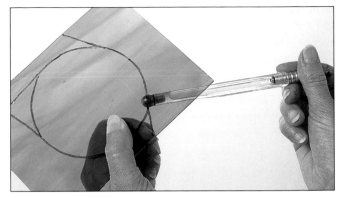
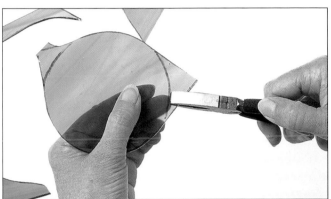

Scoring circles

Circles can be cut using a circle cutter but it is also possible to cut a circle freehand, following the procedure shown above. The suggested scores have been indicated with a felt tip pen; arrows show the direction (top left).

Start the score from the bottom edge of the glass and take it toward and around one side of the required circle (1). When you are near the top of the circle, don't continue around the curve but take the score to the top edge of the glass in a straight line. Place the cutter back on the circle where your previous score left it. Continue around another section of the circle and again score to the edge of the glass (2). Continue in this way until the whole circle is scored.

Now tap the underside of the glass, following the line of the score, to loosen these curved fractures first (top right).

Hold the glass with one hand as shown and place the tip of the pliers next to the score. Grip the glass with the pliers and break away the unwanted sections of glass piece by piece (above left).

Use the pliers to nip away the jagged edges along the score line (above right).

Scoring deep curves

The extra black lines in the middle picture indicate scores that have been made within the deep curve. Score the line of the definitive curve first, then score extra curves within this shape as shown.

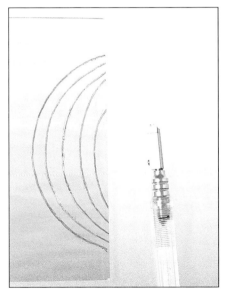

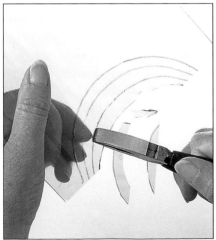

Grip one side of a section with the pliers and gently pull down until you see the score begin to fracture. Move to the other side and repeat. You should now be able to pull out the piece. Carry on until you are left with the required curve.

Grozing

To tidy up the rough edges left on the sides of the glass use the serrated inside jaws of the pliers. Place the jaws over the sides of the glass but don't close them completely. Draw the pliers down or up, removing rough angles and sharp pieces.

Filing or grinding

Dull the sharp edges by rubbing them on a carborundum stone prior to copper foiling. You can also blunt the edges of mirror glass using "wet and dry" sandpaper, wrapped around a block of wood. This is a less abrasive method and less likely to fracture the reflective or mirror side of the glass. Filing also provides a "key" for the copper foil to cling to. Rinse with water and dry the pieces.

Electric grinding machines are much more expensive than carborundum stones and are used for changing the shape of glass as well as smoothing the edges. For a beginner it may be tempting to rely on the grinding machine instead of learning to cut accurately, but although the grinder is very useful, it should be used as an aid rather than a tool. As with all glass work, always wear protective glasses.

ASSEMBLING

Copper foiling

Pull the protective backing off some of the self-adhesive copper tape. Place the edge of the glass in the center of this strip. Now work around the piece, pressing the copper foil onto the edge with your thumb or fingers and ensuring that equal amounts of foil are exposed on either side (below). Overlap the tape where you began and smooth down so the join doesn't show.

Now fold over the excess foil onto the sides of the glass and press down all around the piece. Gently rub and smooth down the foil along the edges and sides with a fid (see bottom picture).

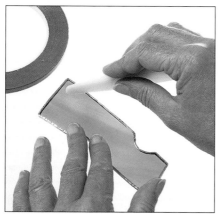

Soldering

Flux must be applied before soldering copper foiled or leaded glass. For copper foil work, apply the liquid flux with a brush. Switch on the soldering iron and wait for it to get hot before starting to solder. This should take less than five minutes.

• Tack soldering

Once all the pieces of your glass are copper foiled and laid out on the pattern ready for soldering, tack solder them first. This simply holds the pieces in place with small blobs of solder. Apply only a dab of flux onto the desired area and melt just a small blob of solder on top, touching the tip of

the iron with the stick of solder and melting a tiny amount onto the foil.

• Tin Soldering

Tin soldering refers to applying a thin, flat amount of solder onto the copper foil to hold the piece together and coat the edges and sides of copper foiled glass.

• Bead soldering

Bead soldering refers to a smooth, slightly rounded flow of solder that is aesthetic rather than essential to copper foiled glass. It disguises the join where two pieces of glass meet. When you have finished tacking, apply flux along all the copper foiled areas. You can bead solder the seams straight away without tinning first.

Hold the iron in one hand and with the other allow the tip of solder to touch the tip of the iron. Draw both slowly along the copper foil in one continuous movement, occasionally touching the stick of solder to melt more as you need it. With a steady hand, move the iron very slowly along, applying just enough solder to form a slightly rounded, smooth seam. Don't "stroke" the iron along the seams, or sharp peaks will form.

Keep the tip of the iron clean by wiping it on a damp sponge from time to time to remove any deposits (see page 11).

It is sufficient to tin solder the back, sides and edges of most projects.

Cleaning stained glass items

Flux is mildly corrosive, and once you have finished soldering a copper foiled piece it is necessary to wash it with warm water and a mild detergent. Wipe the item with a sponge in soapy water and rinse with clear water. Patina can be applied to change the silver color of the solder (see page 11), after which the piece will need to be washed again as above. Always wear rubber gloves when applying patina.

Leading glass

Assembling a window panel using lead is different from the copper foil method. When cutting glass for leaded work, a specific gap must be left between each

piece of glass; this is not necessary for copper foil work. Lead comes in long strips called cames, with a channel on both sides to hold the glass. The center between the channels is called the "heart". You must leave a gap between each piece of glass to accommodate the "heart", which is usually $\frac{1}{16}$" (2 mm) wide. Lead must be stretched before use to strengthen it and straighten out any bends or kinks (see page 11). It is cut to size using the lead knife. If a channel of lead has closed up slightly, it can be re-opened by running the fid along it.

Unlike copper foil, lead only needs to be soldered at the junctions where one piece of lead meets another. Before soldering, the lead junctions are first rubbed with a wire brush to remove oxidization and then with a tallow candle.

With the iron, melt a small amount of solder onto the junctions of lead, just enough to hold them together. Be very careful not to leave the iron on the lead for more than a couple of seconds, otherwise the heat of the iron will melt through the lead, leaving a hole. When you have finished soldering, use the wire brush to clean the joints of lead before the cementing process.

Cementing

Once a lead window panel is assembled, it must be strengthened and weatherproofed with a special lead light putty or cement. It is worked into the lead channels with a brush, filling the gaps between the glass and the lead. When this is done, whiting powder is sprinkled over the panel. This helps to dry the excess cement and makes the glass easier to clean. Both sides of the panel must be cemented, sprinkled with whiting powder and left to "set". Do not leave the cement on for more than about an hour, or it will become too hard to remove. The time will depend, to an extent, on the temperature of the surroundings.

Before the cement is too dry, use the pointed end of a fid to draw down the side of each strip of lead, separating the excess cement from the cement under the lead cames. The panel must then be brushed vigorously in all directions across the cames. This will remove the drying cement from the cames and the glass and will also clean the glass. Change brushes and continue using this method until the cames become darker and cleaner. You may need to draw the fid down the edges of the lead again if some cement seeps out after you have stopped brushing. The cement dries quickly: always keep the lid on the pot when you are not using it to keep the cement moist and workable for next time.

DESIGNING YOUR OWN PIECES

Inspiration for designing your own projects or window panels may come from many sources. Nature books or flower catalogues are full of photographic illustrations for reference if you wish to produce a design of flowers or birds, for example. Look out for ideas that appeal to you and study pictures of both contemporary and traditional stained glass to observe the flow of lines. This may help you to plan your own design. Visit a stained glass supplier and look at the colors of the glass available – they may also prompt an idea.

Designing your own window panel can be one of the most challenging aspects of working in stained glass. Study your design after drawing it onto paper and consider the difficulties you may encounter in cutting the required shapes of glass, remembering the technical limitations imposed by the medium. Start with simple ideas and avoid difficult shapes that will be hard to cut.

If the design of a window panel has a foreground or a central feature, the background has to be thoughtfully constructed. The areas where you will need to put a line to allow for cutting the glass (whether working with copper foil or lead) should be an integral part of the design. You can create either a background grid of diamonds, squares or a backdrop "scene".

The tropical fish panel (page 68) is a good example. The fish shape was drawn using a photograph for inspiration. Use tracing paper to draw on if you want to flip the shape as we did for the fish panel. The fish was then copied several times and arranged as a foreground feature. The background of waves moving across the design created manageable shapes for which glass could be cut easily. Alternatively, sea grasses could have reached from the bottom to the top of the picture. Whichever way you construct it, the background adds strength to the panel.

Avoid too many lines coming together at one point, otherwise you will create a massive, unsightly junction of lead or solder in one area. Consider also the strength of the finished piece. Long, thin shapes with hour glass "waists" will be weak and may break before you have finished making the panel. A design of interrelated shapes and traversing lines will be stronger than a design of parallel lines.

Candle Stand

olored glass comes in an amazing array of textures and colors, some of which are not only effective in windows but are also an ideal choice for decorative objects. This candle stand is made from a glass known as "fractures and streamers". Several varieties in different colors are available. They can have either an opalescent or translucent base, overlaid with pieces and flakes of colored glass fused at a high temperature.

You will need

15 " x 9 " (38 x 22 cm) fractures and streamers glass

black felt tip pen

glass cutter

cutting square

grozer/breaker pliers

carborundum stone

⁷/₃₂ " (5 mm) black-backed copper foil

fid

flux brush

flux

soldering iron

solder

vase cap

rubber gloves

black patina

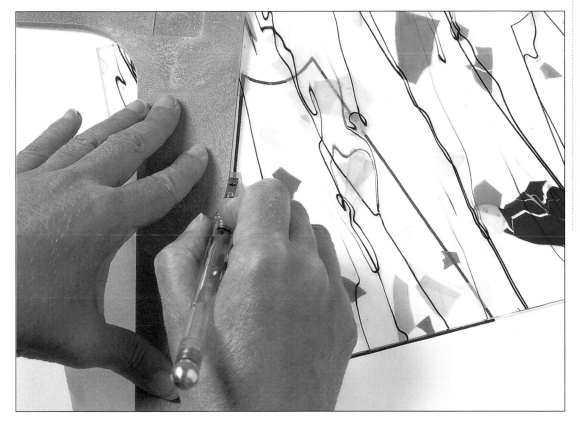

1 Enlarge the templates on page 90 to the correct size and draw over the outlines in black felt tip pen. You will need one large and two small pieces. Lay the glass over the pattern, making sure the lines beneath are clearly visible. Position the cutter correctly (see page 12), align the cutting square and hold it very firmly with one hand while pressing the glass cutter down and along the cutting square, starting at the top. Score each of the straight lines first, breaking the glass after each score. Finally, score and break out the curve at the top of each of the three pieces freehand.

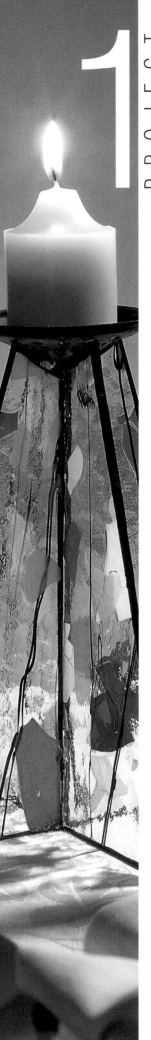

2 Rub the edges of the glass pieces along the carborundum stone to blunt them and provide a "key" for the copper foil. Wash and dry the pieces. Press the edges of the glass centrally onto the adhesive side of the copper foil, leaving equal amounts of foil exposed on either side. Wrap and press down the foil around the edges of each piece, fold the excess down onto the sides of the glass and smooth down with the fid (see page 14).

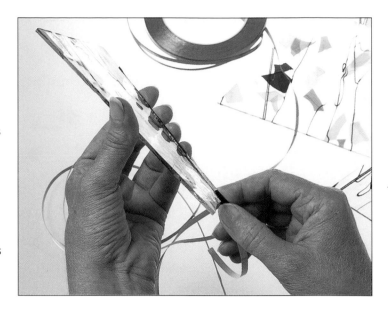

3 Apply flux with a brush and tin solder the copper foiled edges of each piece of glass individually. With a felt tip pen, draw a cross with perfect right angles onto a piece of paper. Place the large central shaft of the stand on one line and one of the "wings" at a right angle, on the marked cross. Melt some solder at the top of this junction to fix the wing in place. Repeat this process with the other wing.

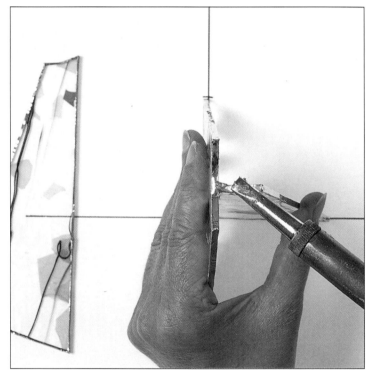

4 When both wings are tack soldered at the top, melt a tiny amount of solder to the bottom edges as shown to secure the sides to the central piece.

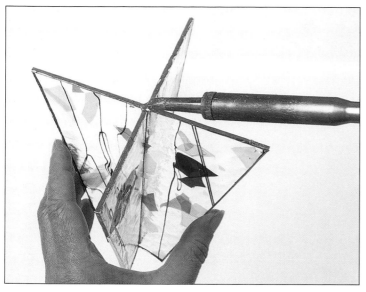

5 Turn the stand upside down and add a tiny amount of solder to the bottom where the sides and the central piece meet. Don't leave any bumps of solder or the stand will rock when it rests on a surface.

6 Turn upright. Place the upturned vase cap into the "cradle" at the top of the stand. Carefully apply flux to the inside edges of the cap and the glass edges beneath and solder the vase cap to the stand.

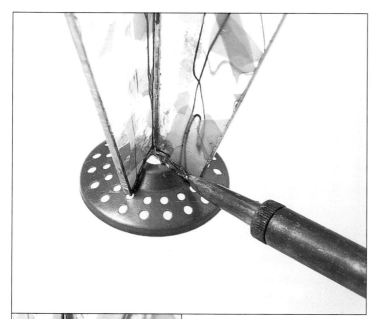

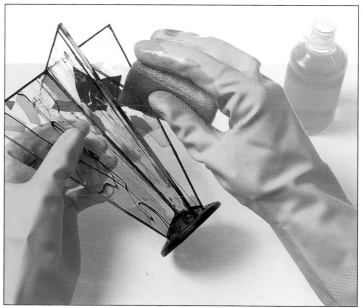

7 Turn the stand upside down and apply a little flux before reinforcing the vase cap to the edges of the stand with some more melted solder.

8 Wash the stand thoroughly in warm soapy water and rinse with clear water to remove the flux. Wearing rubber gloves, tip some black patina onto a sponge and apply it to the soldered copper foiled edges and all over the vase cap. Wash the stand well in warm soapy water and rinse with clear water.

The frame for this small mirror has been drawn freehand to create a deliberately irregular shape. Two shades of opalescent glass have been used here, but you can use any number of colors. Many stained glass studios which also act as suppliers have scrap bins of off-cuts – the small, irregular leftovers of glass. Sold by the pound and less expensive than larger, regular sheets of glass, they are ideal for imaginative use in small projects.

You will need

8 " x 8 " (20.5 x 20.5 cm)
pale green opalescent glass

8 " x 8 " (20.5 x 20.5 cm)
medium green opalescent glass

6 " x 6 " (15.5 x 15.5 cm)
mirror glass, $\frac{1}{16}$ " (2 mm) thick

scissors

felt tip pen

glass cutter

grozer/breaker pliers

carborundum stone

$\frac{7}{32}$ " (5 mm) copper foil

fid

flux brush

flux

soldering iron

solder

cutting square

$\frac{5}{8}$ " (16 mm) copper foil

10 " (25 cm) copper wire or
picture wire for hanging

sponge

1 Enlarge and make two copies of the template on page 90 and cut out the shapes for the border from one of them. Lay these templates on top of the glass and draw around with a fine felt tip pen. Leave some space around each shape.

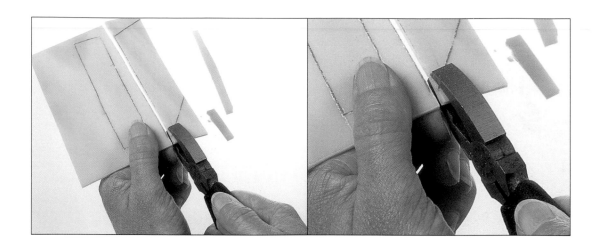

2 Score along the black lines with the glass cutter, always taking the score from one side of the glass to the other. Narrow strips of glass may be easier to break using pliers. Hold them next to the score and snap the glass apart. Cut out all of the shapes and lay them out on the pattern to check that they fit accurately. File the edges of the glass on the carborundum stone, rinse and dry each piece and then carefully and neatly wrap the edges in the copper foil. Smooth down the foil with a fid.

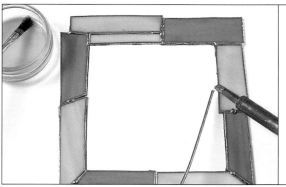 

3 Place the copper foiled pieces onto the pattern, brush with flux and tack solder in place. Apply more flux before bead soldering the seams where two pieces of glass meet. Tin solder the side edges as shown in picture. Be careful not to apply too much solder or it will run over the sides and form lumps. Turn the frame over and tin solder the back, then lift the frame into a vertical position and tin solder the inside and outside edges of the frame.

4 If necessary, measure and mark the size of the mirror with a felt tip pen on the reflective side of the mirror glass. The size of the mirror should be larger than the aperture within the frame. Score straight lines using the cutting square. Gently rub the mirror edges on the carborundum stone (careful - they fracture easily), rinse with water and dry.

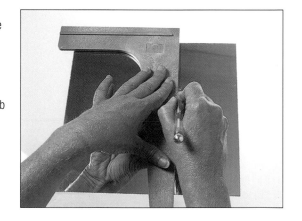

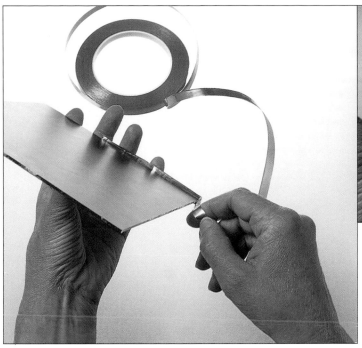

5 Copper foil the mirror using ⅝" (16 mm) foil, leaving equal amounts of foil exposed on either side. Overlap the foil where you began and fold the excess onto both sides of the mirror before smoothing it down with the fid. Apply flux and tin solder the edges of the mirror before washing it thoroughly to remove any remaining flux.

6 Lay the mirror, reflective side down, onto the back of the frame. Now attach the mirror to the frame by melting a little solder at a time to join the edges of the mirror to all the seams of the frame beneath.

7 Measure and cut a length of picture wire or copper wire and solder it into one of the seams at the top of the frame, at the back. It will be necessary to hold the wire in place with pliers as it will become too hot to hold with your fingers. Pull the wire across over the top of the mirror and down the other side, and solder it into one of the seams of the frame in the same way. Use a damp sponge to clean the soldered areas of flux.

Etching is a very satisfying way to decorate the surface of clear or tinted glass. With the application of etching cream it is possible to achieve a subtle frosted effect. Always read the manufacturer's label carefully, wear rubber gloves and work in a well-ventilated room. A variety of materials can be used as resist or protective coating to keep some areas of the glass clear. This project uses wood glue with great effect. The plain glass coasters with polished sides were purchased from a large department store. You may find other shapes that can be decorated in the same manner.

You will need

4 round glass coasters (from department stores)

16 small glass nuggets

wood glue

masking tape

scissors

fid or plastic implement

plastic bowl

rubber gloves

etching cream

U.V. glue

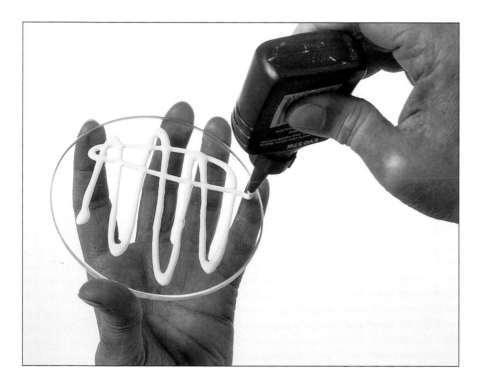

1 Clean the coasters thoroughly. Practice squeezing the wood glue onto some paper until you have control of the flow. Start by touching the nozzle of the bottle on the glass, and as you squeeze the glue out lift the bottle and apply a wavy line of glue from side to side in a fairly swift movement. When you reach the bottom, change direction and carry on applying the glue as shown. It will wash off if you want to start again. Decorate all coasters in this way and leave to dry for about 3-4 hours.

2 Carefully apply masking tape to the edge of each coaster, making sure it does not go over the edge onto the flat surface where the glue has been applied. Rub down the masking tape onto the edges and the back so it is completely flattened.

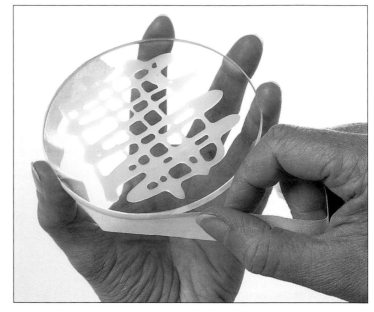

3 Protect the underside of the coasters with strips of masking tape and make sure there are no gaps. Rub and smooth the tape down well.

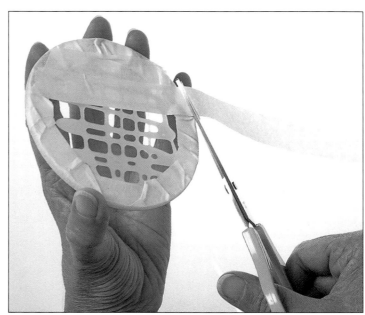

artist's tip

If you leave the glue on for longer than a day, it will harden and cannot easily be removed. If this happens, soak the coasters in warm water until the glue softens, then rub it off with a sponge.

4 Carefully read the manufacturer's instructions on the etching cream container. Wearing rubber gloves, put the pot of cream and a coaster into a plastic bowl. A plastic implement such as a fid can be used to apply and spread the cream onto the surface of the coaster. Leave for about 15 minutes. Wearing rubber gloves, rinse off the cream under cold water until it is completely removed. Remove the masking tape and use a sponge to rub off the glue or peel it off with your fingers. Leave the coasters to dry.

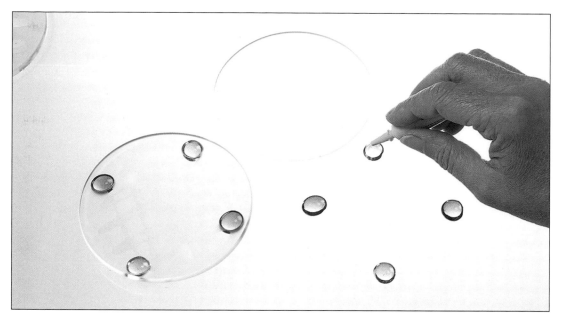

5 Lay out the small glass nuggets, flat side up, and check their position by laying a coaster onto the nuggets. When you are happy with the position, take off the coaster and put to one side. Squeeze a tiny amount of glass bonding glue onto the center of the nuggets. It should not completely cover the nugget, otherwise it will be flooded when you lay the coaster on top.

6 Lay the coaster etched side down onto the nuggets and lightly press down. Leave to set. U.V. glue should become firm very quickly if there is plenty of natural light, but leave the coasters undisturbed for a couple of hours to be entirely sure.

variation

For a subtly spotted coaster like this one, tiny self-adhesive circular labels can be used as resists. There are many other shapes available, for example stars (for a seasonal look) or hearts (for that special Valentine present). To remove the labels, simply soak the coasters in warm water and rub the resists off with a sponge. Differently colored nuggets were used for this coaster.

4

Blue & Silver Picture Frame

imple shapes can sometimes be surprisingly difficult to attain. Practise cutting the long sharp angles in this project with some clear glass first. Although a single color was used for this frame, a glass with an interesting texture or pattern, such as "fracture and streamers" glass, would make a good alternative.

12 " x 12 " (30 x 30 cm) blue antique or semi-antique glass

clear picture glass, ¹⁄₁₆ " (2 mm) thick

glass cutter

cutting square

carborundum stone

⁷⁄₃₂ " (5 mm) silver-backed copper foil

fid

flux brush

flux

soldering iron

solder

fine copper wire

galvanized wire or thick copper wire

round-nosed pliers

thin card

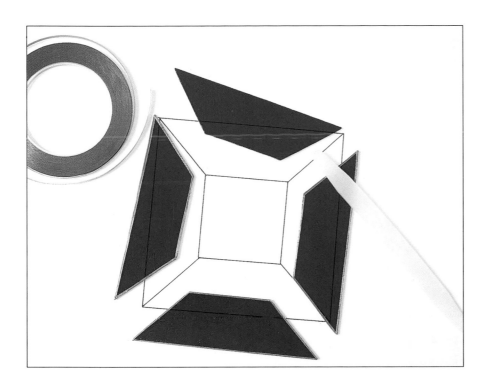

1 Enlarge the template on page 90 to the correct size and place the transparent glass over it. Accurately cut out each piece of the frame, using the cutting square for neat straight edges. Lay the pieces back onto the template before copper foiling to check each angle butts up to its neighbor without a gap. Cut a square of clear glass for the center. Carefully file every piece of blue glass and the square for the center, rinse with water and dry. Copper foil each piece and smooth the foil onto the edges and sides of the glass with the fid. Place all the pieces onto the template.

2 Apply a dab of flux to each corner with a brush before tack soldering the pieces together. Now apply flux to all the copper foil and bead solder all the seams. Aim for a smooth, slightly raised "bead" of solder along these joins.

3 Lift the frame into an upright position and tin solder the edges. You can use up any blobs of solder that have accumulated along the outside edge and smooth them out with the iron along the sides of the frame. Lay the frame facedown and tin solder the back.

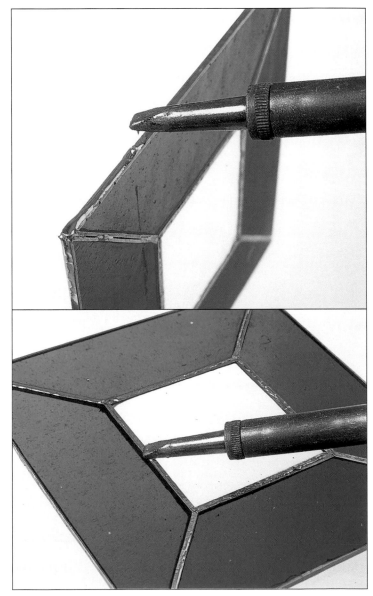

4 Snip off four pieces of copper wire, about ¾" (2 cm) in length, and curl the ends using a pair of round-nosed pliers. Position the pieces of wire with the curls over the clear glass and the tails along the seams of all four corners of the frame. Apply a dab of flux with the brush and then carefully melt a tiny amount of solder to fix the wires to the seams beneath.

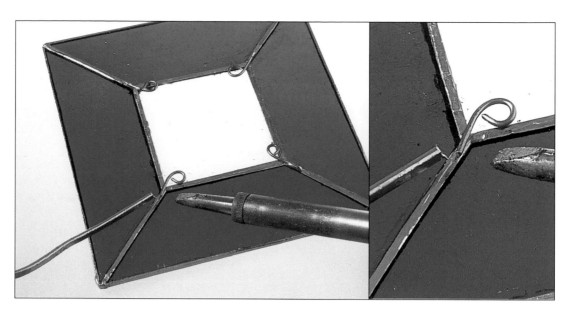

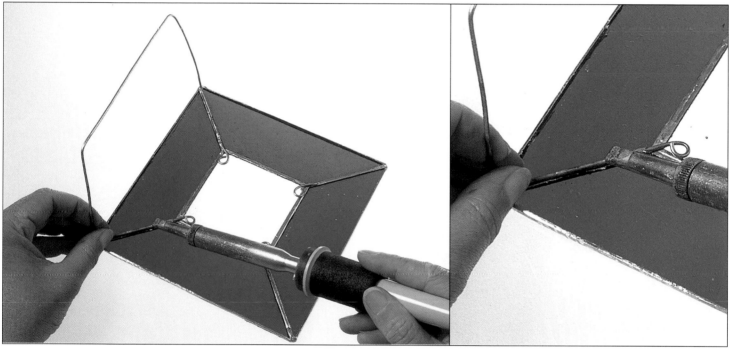

5 For the stand, bend the galvanized wire into a "U"-shape using the pliers. Manipulate one end to an angle so that it aligns with the diagonal seam in one bottom corner of the frame. Apply some flux and solder into place. Manipulate the other end in the same way and solder onto the other seam. Once it is soldered in place, the stand can still be gently adjusted until you are satisfied with the angle of the frame. Wash it carefully in warm soapy water and rinse with clear water. Cut a piece of thin card the same size as the plain glass square and use this as a template to cut out a favorite photograph. Gently lift the copper tabs and slip the photograph, facedown, and card onto the clear glass. The tabs can then be pressed back into place to hold the picture and card firmly against the glass.

This simple project is good for practicing how to cut straight lines and other skills such as copper foiling and soldering. For a good result always check that everything fits well at each stage of the making process. You could use differently colored or opalescent glass instead of the streaky cathedral for a different effect.

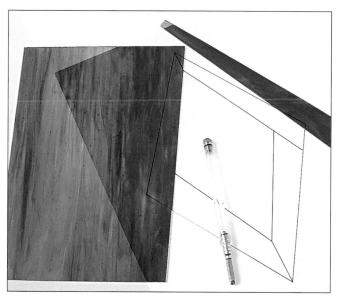

1 Enlarge the template on page 91 to the correct size and make three copies of it. Use one to cut out the diamond mirror shape, place this on the reflective side of the mirror and draw around it with the felt tip pen. Score and break the mirror glass, using the cutting square to achieve a straight line. If the colored glass for the frame is transparent, lay it over the second photocopied template, score, using the square again, and break. If the glass is opaque, cut out the four sides of the frame and proceed as for the mirror.

2 Once all the pieces are cut and fit together well when laid out on the pattern, gently rub the edges of the glass on the carborundum stone to smooth it and provide a "key" for the copper foil. Be careful with the mirror glass: too much rubbing will cause chips or fractures.

3 Rinse and dry all pieces. Pull back the backing from the copper foil and press the edge of one piece of glass down in the center, leaving equal amounts of foil exposed on either side. Continue pressing down the foil around the mirror and overlap where you began. Fold the foil over onto the sides of the glass and smooth down using the fid. Repeat for all other pieces. Place the side panels of the sconce and the mirror with the reflective side up onto the template. Check for a good fit: there should be no gaps between the pieces. Apply dabs of flux and tack solder together.

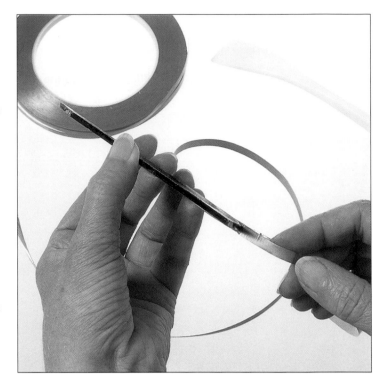

4 Apply flux with a brush along all the copper foil and start to bead solder the joints. Melt the solder with the tip of the iron and move slowly along the seams, allowing the solder to form a smooth and slightly raised "bead" of solder. Tin solder the sides, back and edges of the sconce.

5 Cut a short piece of wire and bend it into a loop, leaving two short ends. Lay the mirror face down and position the ends of the wire loop onto the vertical seam at the top of the mirror sconce. Add a dab of flux with a brush and melt some solder onto the ends to secure them to the seam below.

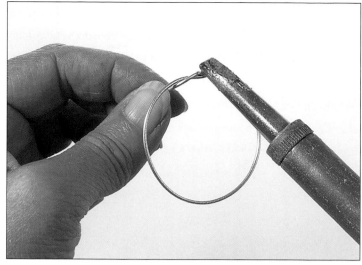

6 Wrap the end of a piece of silver-coated or fine gauge galvanized wire, approximately 11 " (28 cm) long, around a tea light and overlap. Hold in place and remove the tea light.

7 Twist the overlap around the rest of the circle now formed. Melt a small amount of solder to hold this twisted wire in place.

8 With the pliers, hold the long end of the wire and bend it at a right angle under the wire circle. Check that the tea light will not fall out of this "cradle" and adjust if necessary.

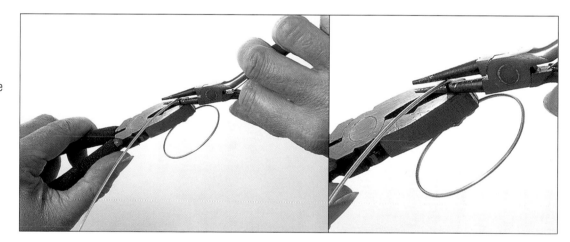

9 Bend the wire back and down as shown and trim the wire to fit onto the vertical seam directly below the mirror. Melt some solder with the iron so the wire blends into the seam of solder beneath. Wash the sconce carefully in warm soapy water and rinse. Rest a tea light in the cradle and, if necessary, adjust the wire so the tea light is level.

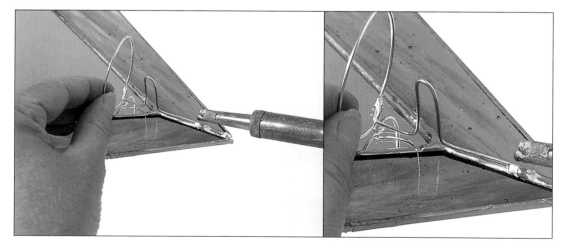

A s in many of the projects in this book, the selection of colors and type of glass is up to you. For this project, each piece of transparent glass that makes up the box is a different color, creating an interesting effect when viewed from different angles and also when the lid is shut. You may want to use just one color or a combination of two. Before assembling the box, try different color combinations until you are satisfied with the overall effect.

You will need

6 " x 6 " (15.5 x 15.5 cm) each of lime green, lilac, pale blue, turquoise and pale yellow cathedral (corrella) glass

glass cutter

cutting square

grozer/breaker pliers

plasticine

carborundum stone

$\frac{7}{32}$ " (5 mm) silver-backed copper foil

fid

soldering iron

solder

flux brush

flux

felt tip pen

pins with ceramic heads (available from fabric store)

silver-coated wire

1 Make two copies of the templates on page 92. Lay the glass onto the templates, score and break it using the cutting square for perfectly straight edges. Lay the pieces onto the spare pattern and check each piece is accurate.

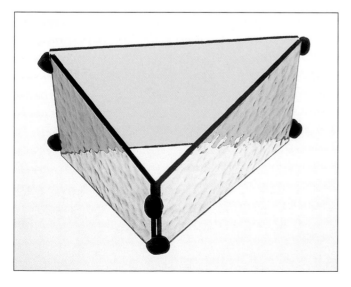

2 Assemble the sides of the box prior to foiling to check the sizes and shapes of the pieces are correct and to see if the colors you have chosen work well together. Small lumps of plasticine squeezed onto the edges of the glass will help to hold the pieces in position. When you are satisfied with the composition, rub the edges of the glass on the carborundum stone to blunt them and provide a "key" for the copper foil. Rinse the pieces with water and dry. Copper foil all the rectangular pieces and smooth down the foil with the fid.

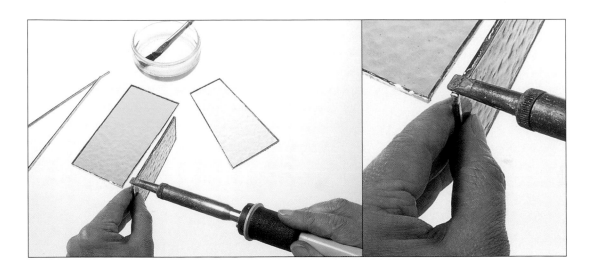

3 Brush the edges with flux and tin solder each piece of glass individually on the front, back and sides of the copper foil.

4 Assemble the three sides by tack soldering the top and bottom corners of each vertical. Tin solder all the seams.

5 Lift the assembled sides and place on top of the triangular piece cut for the bottom. Check that it fits neatly: the only areas that should protrude are the corners. Mark these small points with a felt tip pen as shown. Do the same for the lid.

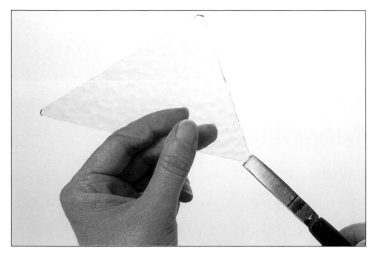

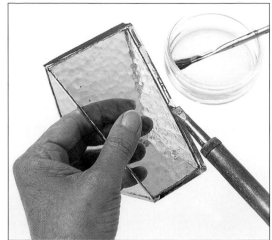

6 Nip off the sharp points of both pieces with the pliers: place the tip of the pliers onto the corners, squeeze and nip them away. The insides of the pliers are serrated, and placing them over the corners and not closing them completely while making a downward movement will also remove these points. Gently rub the edges on the carborundum stone, wash the pieces and dry.

7 Copper foil the base and lid and tin solder both. Now brush all the seams with a little flux and tin solder the base and sides together.

8 To make the lid, hold one pin in place very steadily on the back edge of the lid as shown. Allow the pin head to protrude slightly. Be very careful not to burn yourself with the soldering iron. Add a very small amount of solder to tack the pin in place. When this is done, remove your finger and add a little more solder to cover the pin. Allow the glass and solder to cool down for a few minutes, then do the other hinge.

9 Cut a piece of silver wire approximately the length of the box height. Center the wire over the pin just next to the ceramic head and bend over so that the ends come together. Bend one end around the pin once more and then twist the ends around each other or nip them together. Position the lid on top of the box and make sure it is flush with the sides. Dab the dangling twisted wire ends with flux and carefully solder them to the side seam of the box. Still holding the lid carefully in place, attach the other hinge in the same way. Wash the box thoroughly in warm soapy water and rinse.

stained glass/project 6

Wild Creations
Gallery

Sweetheart mirror
Artist: Barbara Seward, Redford Studios
Irregularly-sized circles cut from opalescent glass have been copper foiled and soldered to a heart mirror. A chain is soldered to the back for hanging. The top of the heart is cut as a curve instead of the more difficult "V" shape.

Candle lamp
Artist: Ben Essex
The shade of this pretty candle lamp is three-sided. Each of the flat panels was made individually before being assembled to make the shade. The stand is made of three pieces of wire, tied together with wire and soldered in the middle. The feet were curled with jewelry pliers and the top ends of wire bent apart to make space for a tea light.

Flower vase
Transparent colored glass, copper foiled and soldered, can be assembled into simple and elegant containers for the home. Remember that these items should not be filled with water or used to store food.

Ornamental frame
Various differently sized, copper foiled nuggets are soldered onto a square glass bevel, forming an unusual frame. Small wire tabs soldered to the back, hold the picture in place.

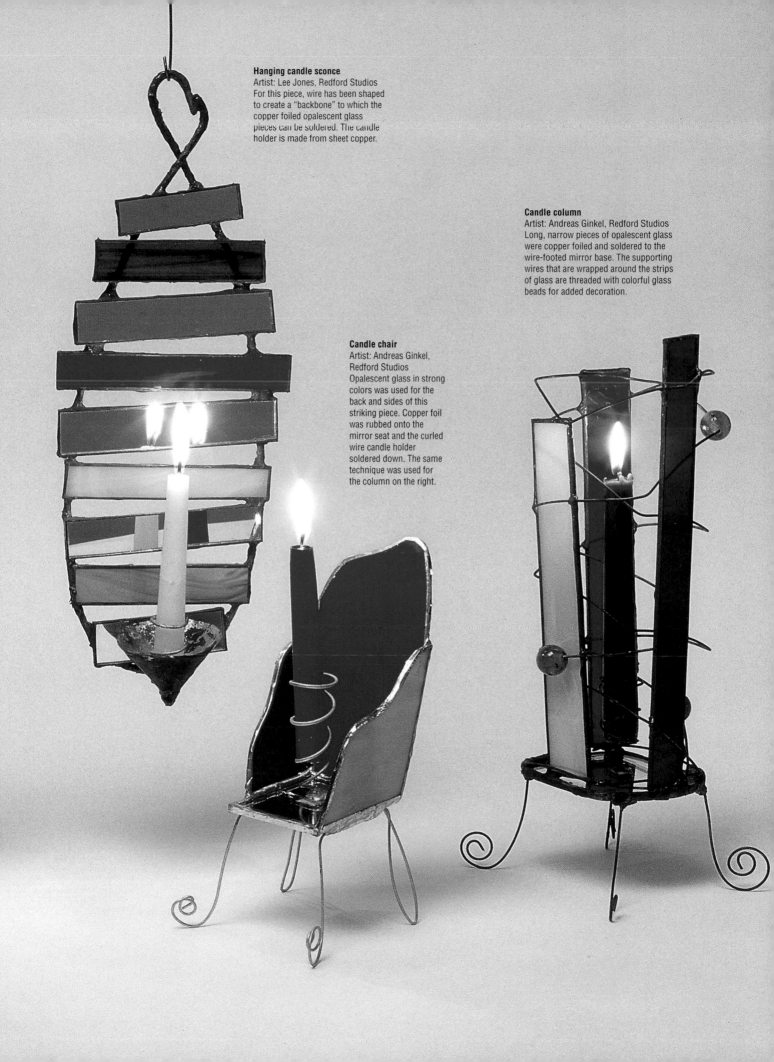

Hanging candle sconce
Artist: Lee Jones, Redford Studios
For this piece, wire has been shaped to create a "backbone" to which the copper foiled opalescent glass pieces can be soldered. The candle holder is made from sheet copper.

Candle column
Artist: Andreas Ginkel, Redford Studios
Long, narrow pieces of opalescent glass were copper foiled and soldered to the wire-footed mirror base. The supporting wires that are wrapped around the strips of glass are threaded with colorful glass beads for added decoration.

Candle chair
Artist: Andreas Ginkel, Redford Studios
Opalescent glass in strong colors was used for the back and sides of this striking piece. Copper foil was rubbed onto the mirror seat and the curled wire candle holder soldered down. The same technique was used for the column on the right.

7 PROJECT Pressed Flower Mobile

Think about using the transparency of glass and the flexible medium of copper foil in unexpected ways. Copper foil allows for creative freedom and the ability to assemble and solder many objects. The gallery on page 56 of pressed flowers in glass by Janice Issitt shows good examples. Be careful not to allow flowers to be exposed to too much direct sunlight, however, or their colors will fade. In this mobile the flowers are held between $1/16$ " (2 mm) glass and glass bevels, cut pieces of clear glass with polished faceted edges.

You will need

3 square glass bevels,
3 " x 3 " (7.5 x 7.5 cm)

clear glass, $1/16$ " (2 mm)
thick, large enough to cut out
3 bevel-sized squares

piece of paper

fine felt tip or other pen

glass cutter

cutting square

carborundum stone

assortment of pressed flowers

$5/8$ " (8 mm) copper foil

fid

silver-plated wire or silver
jump rings (available from
jewelry suppliers)

round-nosed pliers

flux brush

flux

soldering iron

solder

sponge

1 Place a bevel onto a piece of paper and carefully draw around the edge with a fine-tipped pen. Draw around each bevel individually. Use these templates to cut pieces of clear glass to exactly the same size as the corresponding bevels. File the edges of each piece of glass very carefully so as not to cause a fracture. Rinse and dry thoroughly. Make sure each piece is perfectly clean.

2 Study the assortment of flowers you have and choose one or more for each bevel. Arrange the flowers onto the clear glass pieces and place the corresponding bevel on top.

3 For each piece, squeeze the glass and the bevel together tightly so the flowers cannot slip and neatly copper foil the edges. Rub the foil down very firmly onto the sides of the glass. Continue to foil each square of glass and glass bevel.

4 You may choose to buy jump rings for the links that hold the squares of glass together. If you use silver-plated wire, wind it around the end of a round pencil or similar-sized implement – I used a flux brush.

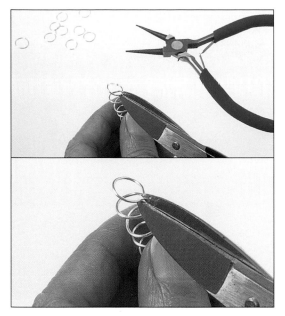

5 To make the rings, snip each loop at the bottom where the wires cross. You will need sixteen rings in total.

6 Flux and tin solder the copper foil around the glass squares. Lay them on the table in a position where you can comfortably hold the silver rings to the soldered edges (such as on top of another bevel). Use the round-nosed pliers to hold each ring steady while you carefully add a drop of solder to secure the ring to the square. Attach two loops to the top and bottom of the first and second square and two loops to the top only of the third. Clean each square gently with a dampened soapy sponge.

7 Now link the glass squares together with the spare silver loops. Close and solder the linking loops carefully. Adding these loops requires patience and a gentle touch, so take your time.

Alternative design:

Pressed flower jewelry

Designer and maker: Janice Issitt

For beautiful glass jewelry, cut pairs of very small glass rectangles, place tiny pressed flowers between the glass and copper foil and solder the glass together.

Petal Picture Frame

O palescent glass can reflect light which makes it an ideal choice for objects that do not require a light source behind them to enhance their color. It often is not one pure color: a mixture of colors, though subtle, spreads across the sheet, giving it life and movement. The opacity of different types of opalescent glass can also vary. The glass used for this project is slightly transparent, allowing the template to be seen through the glass.

You will need

6 " x 6 " (15.5 x 15.5 cm) pale amber wispy opalescent glass

6 " x 6 " (15.5 x 15.5 cm) purple wispy opalescent glass

6 " x 6 " (15.5 x 15.5 cm) clear glass, 1⁄16 " (2 mm) thick

glass cutter

grozer/breaker pliers

carborundum stone

7⁄32 " (5 mm) silver-backed copper foil

fid

flux brush

flux

soldering iron

solder

copper wire, 1 mm (gauge 18) and 1.5 mm (gauge 16)

round-nosed pliers

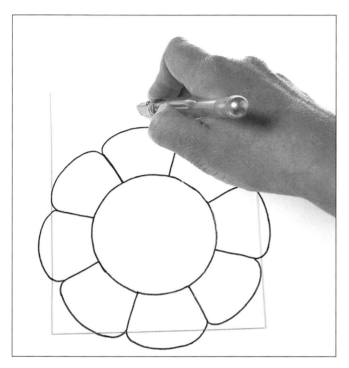

1 Enlarge and make two copies of the pattern on page 90. Place the clear glass on top of one of them and start to score the center circle. Begin the score at the bottom of the glass and move the cutter upward and around half of the circle. Don't try to continue around the bend but take the score straight towards the top edge of the piece of glass first. Now place the cutter back on the circle where the first score moved away. Continue to score around some more of the circle and score to the edge of the glass again. Continue in this way until the entire circle is scored.

2 Hold the glass firmly with one hand and place the pliers next to the score. Break the glass, piece by piece, until you are left with a circle.

3 Some sharp points of glass will remain protruding from the circle. Place the tip of the pliers onto the glass, squeeze them shut and nip off these tiny pieces. Carry on around the circle, removing all sharp points in the same way.

4 Gently file the edge of the circle on the carborundum stone. Don't rub too vigorously or the glass will fracture. If any tiny chips do occur, they will be covered up by the copper foil.

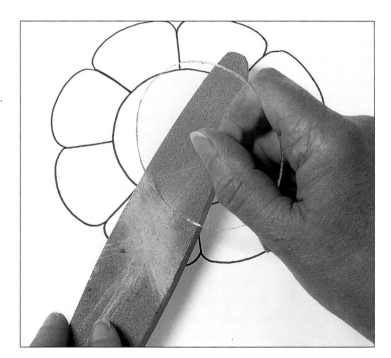

artist's tip
Any drops of solder that fall onto the glass when you're tin soldering the edges of the petal frame can be removed later by picking them off with your fingers once they are cool.

5 Score and break all the petals, on the colored glass. Remove any sharp points using the pliers in the same way as in step 3 to obtain the gentle curves of the petals. File the edges of the petals on the carborundum stone and rinse with water. Dry and copper foil all petals and the center circle.

6 Place the pieces back on the pattern. Tack solder them first, then bead solder the front seams neatly. Turn the frame over and tin solder the back as shown. Lift the frame into a vertical position and tin solder around the edges of the frame.

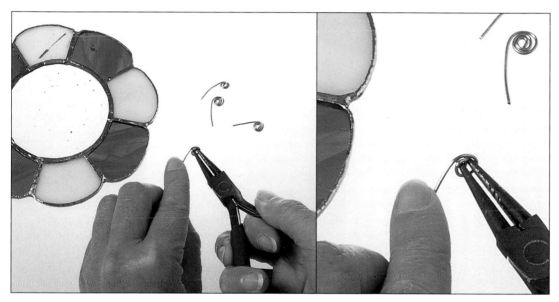

7 Snip off four pieces of 1 mm (18 gauge) copper wire, approximately ½" to ⅝" (1.2 to 1.5 cm) long. To make the small copper "tabs" that will hold the picture in place, grasp one end of the wire with the round-nosed pliers and curl the wire inward. Flux and solder the straight end of each tab along a seam on the back of the frame so the curl protrudes over the clear glass center.

8 To make a stand, cut a piece of 1.5 mm (16 gauge) copper wire, approximately 10 ¼" (26 cm) long. Hold the wire near the center with your hands spaced about 4 " (10 cm) apart, and bend at right angles. Lay flat and bend about 1 " to 2 " (2.5 to 3 cm) of the wire ends upward. Manipulate one end into a slight curve and place it onto the curved seam between the petals and the circle. Melt solder along the wire to fix it to the seam. Do the same with the other end. Be very careful not to touch your fingers with the soldering iron. Gently wash the frame in warm soapy water and rinse with clear water. You can adjust the stand by manipulating the wire until you are satisfied with the angle of the frame.

C opper foil is ideal for creating three-dimensional objects using colored or mirror glass. This project shows how to make a box or cube and also explains how others can be added on, creating a triple container for candles. The boxes are decorated with a black contour paste or outliner, also available in silver and gold, which is available from stained glass suppliers or craft shops.

You will need

24 " x 24 " (61 x 61 cm) transparent pink cathedral glass

piece of paper

black felt tip pen

set square

glass cutter

cutting square

grozer/breaker pliers

carborundum stone

copper foil

fid

flux brush

flux

soldering iron

solder

round-nosed jewelry pliers

galvanized steel wire, 1.5 mm (16 gauge)

black patina

protective gloves

black contour paste

3 tea lights

1 With a black felt tip pen, and using a set square, draw a square of the desired size – the one shown here is approximately 2 ⅛" x 2 ⅛" (5.4 x 5.4 cm) – onto a piece of white paper. Place the glass over the template and score, using the cutting square for perfectly straight sides, following the lines beneath. Remember that you will have to cut 12 individual, identically sized squares from your sheet of glass.

2 The glass can be snapped apart with the help of the pliers. Hold the glass firmly and place your hand and the pliers very close to either side of the score. Gently rub the sides of the glass along the carborundum stone, rinse off the dust and dry. Copper foil each piece.

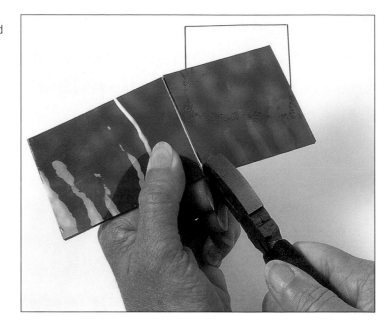

3 Apply flux to the edges of each individual square and tin solder the back and front but leave the sides solder free. Once all squares are tinned, carefully assemble the boxes. Begin by placing two squares together, butting up the sides against one another at right angles, hold steadily and place a tiny amount of melted solder onto the top and bottom corners.

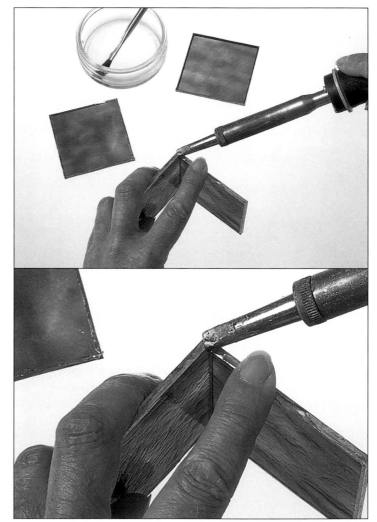

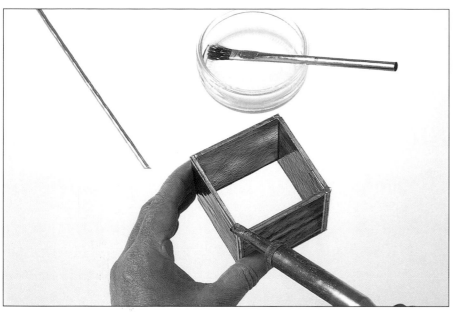

4 Add the third and the fourth square in the same way. Ensure that the box is square and neat. Be careful not to burn your fingers with the soldering iron.

5 Turn the cube onto its side and apply enough solder along each seam to cover the join.

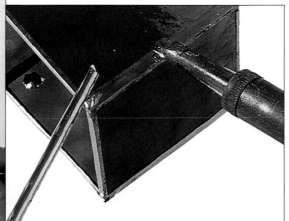

6 To make a base for each cube, place each one individually onto a piece of white paper. With a fine felt tip pen, draw along the inside edges of each cube and use these templates for scoring and breaking three individual base pieces.

stained glass/project 9

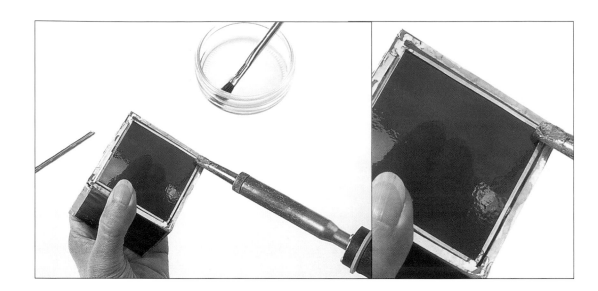

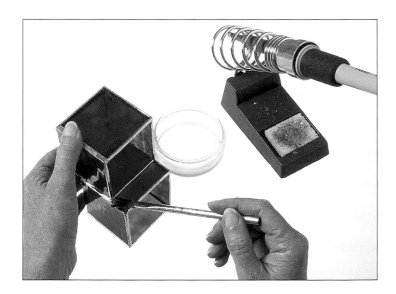

7 Blunt the edges, rinse, dry and copper foil each base piece neatly. Smooth the copper foil down with a fid. Place the base into one end of its corresponding cube, keeping it flush with the sides. Tack solder the corners to hold it in place. Melt more solder along the seams to cover the joins, keeping the soldering smooth. Do the same with the other two boxes.

8 Wash and dry the boxes. Place one box on its side and position the second one as shown, with the opening facing the same way. Hold it carefully as you tack solder it into place. Neatly solder down the side seams. Lay the two boxes flat on their sides and add the third box in the same way.

9 Cut eight lengths of approximately 3 ½" (9 cm) galvanized steel or other strong, flexible wire and curl the ends with round-nosed pliers.

10 In order to give the legs a level footing, begin by fluxing and soldering one leg to a corner of the highest cube. Now add the remaining legs to all the corners, keeping the curled feet all at approximately the same level, so the candle holder will stand straight. You can always give the feet another twist with the pliers.

11 Wearing rubber gloves, apply black patina to the seams and the wire legs. Wash the candle holder in warm soapy water and then rinse. When it is completely dry, apply a spiral of black contour paste and allow to dry.

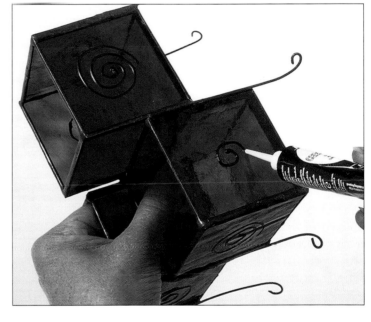

variation

Instead of a triple candle holder, you can, of course, make individual ones, too. Choose a different color, such as this fresh green, for a different effect.

Clocks, Mirrors and Picture Frames
Gallery

Pieces by Janice Issitt

These items are made using copper foiling and soldering. The borders are made in the same way, sandwiching pressed flowers between two pieces of clear glass.

A pretty mixture of flowers are pressed between two layers of clear glass for the border of this hanging mirror.

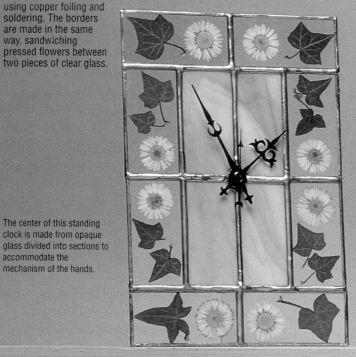

The center of this standing clock is made from opaque glass divided into sections to accommodate the mechanism of the hands.

Fuchsia flowers and leaves frame this standing mirror.

Made with copper foil as are all the items here, this standing mirror has a border of ivy leaves and verbena flowers.

A pretty picture frame of ferns with the solder treated with copper sulphate for a warm coppery finish.

A hanging picture frame using a variety of pressed flowers and leaves. The links for the chain have been soldered to the vertical lines of solder for strength.

A standing clock with pressed narcissi flowers which coordinate with the color of the center panel.

The solder on this mirror made from opalescent glass has been treated with a copper sulphate patina.

The border of this standing mirror is offset with oblong shapes of clear glass containing a mixture of various leaves and flowers.

When cutting glass for this leaded window, it is important to make allowance for the central section – the "heart" – of each lead came. This "heart" is usually ¹⁄₁₆" (2 mm) wide, and the glass must be cut leaving a gap between all pieces to accommodate it. Draw the pattern using a medium felt tip pen which produces a line the same width as the "heart". Panels made with lead are treated with a weatherproofing putty or cement in the final stages which makes them the most suitable choice for external windows.

You will need

6 " x 8 " (15.5 x 20.5 cm) of lilac, yellow, turquoise, aqua, green and pink cathedral glass

2 yellow roundels, approximately 2 ¾ " (7 cm) in diameter

medium felt tip pen

glass cutter

cutting square

grozer/breaker pliers

1 length of ⅜ " (1 cm) "H" lead

1 length of ¼ " (6 mm) "H" lead

flat wooden board, at least 16 " x 12 " (40 x 30 cm)

2 wooden 1 " x 1 " (2.5 x 2.5 cm) battens, one approximately 15 " (38 cm), the other 10 ¼ " (26 cm) long

ruler

pencil

small hammer

nails

lead knife

12 horseshoe nails

wire brush

tallow candle

soldering iron

solder

lead light cement (specialist putty)

fid

rubber gloves

whiting

brush

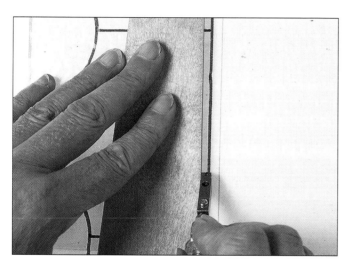

1 Enlarge the template on page 91 to the correct size and make an additional copy. Redraw all the inside lines on the template with the medium felt tip pen to indicate the ¹⁄₁₆ " (2 mm) width of the "heart". Lay the differently colored pieces of glass, one after the other, onto one of the templates to score. Always place the wheel of the glass cutter on the inside of the "cut" line. Use a cutting square for the straight lines. Score and break all the pieces.

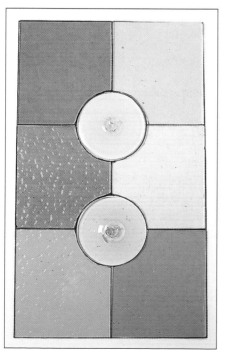

2 Either use the colors shown here or follow your own arrangement. When all the pieces of glass are cut and laid out onto the spare pattern, you should be able to see the felt tip pen lines between each piece. Now prepare the lead by stretching it to remove any kinks and bends. Use either a lead vice, fixed to a sturdy table, or ask someone to help you (see page 11). Pull the lead until you feel it "give" and straighten.

3 With a ruler, measure half the width of the wider lead. This is the distance at which you will have to draw a perimeter line all around the spare template. Lay the template onto the flat wooden board and nail down the two battens alongside the perimeter line you have just drawn. The battens must form a right angle in one corner of the template. Please note that if you are making this panel for a specific site you will need to draw the perimeter line according to your measurements for the site (see artist's tip).

4 Lay the wider lead along the longer batten and mark it with the end of the lead knife where it crosses the perimeter line at the top of the template. Mark another length of lead for the width of the panel.

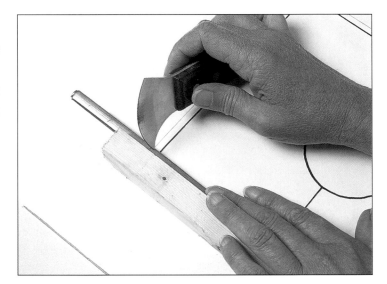

5 Now cut the lead to the correct size by placing the blade of the knife on top of the lead and slowly but firmly pressing it down while rocking the blade from side to side. Pushing down too fast will cause the lead to crush or twist beneath the blade.

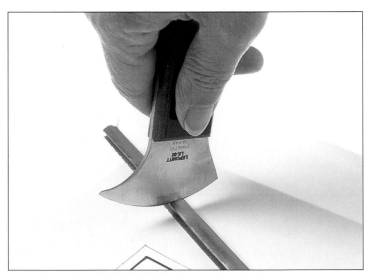

6 When you have cut the two strips of outside lead, lay them along the battens and pin each exposed end in place with a horseshoe nail. Use the handle of the lead knife to tap them into place. Position the first piece of glass by slotting it into the channels of the lead as shown.

artist's tip

Running the fid along the inside of the channel of lead will open any crushed or closed areas.

7 For the leading inside the panel, cut the required pieces of the stretched narrower lead and place them into position on the straight sides of the glass. Mark the lead at the correct length before cutting. Remember to make an allowance for the adjoining piece of lead as shown.

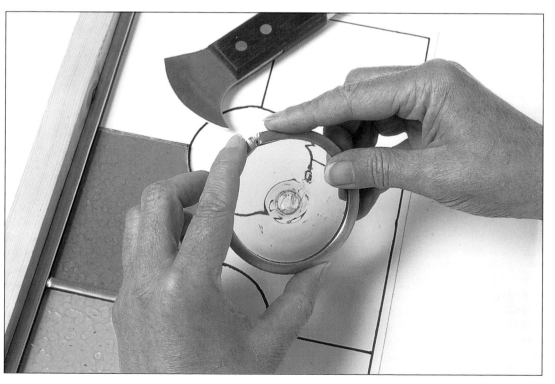

8 Measure and cut a piece of narrow lead for the glass roundel and wrap it around, making sure the edges of the circle are well tucked into the lead channels.

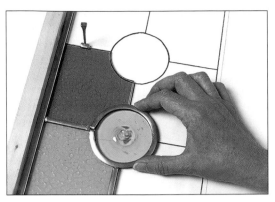

9 Place the leaded roundel onto the board and push it in position next to the glass. Ensure that the glass fits snugly into the lead came of the roundel.

10 Continue placing the glass and lead, building up the panel. Tap in horseshoe nails as you work to hold the glass and lead in place. Place scraps of lead between the glass and the horseshoe nails and tap them firmly into place. This prevents pieces that are already in position from slipping out while you continue working.

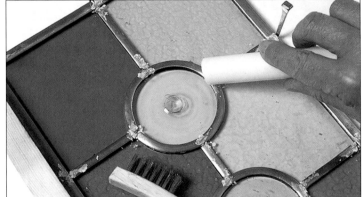

11 Rub across each lead joint with a wire brush, then rub the joints with the tallow candle in preparation for soldering. Switch on the iron.

12 Very carefully apply a small amount of solder onto each joint. Don't leave the iron on the lead for more than a few seconds as the iron can melt the lead beneath, leaving a hole. When you have completed one side, turn the panel over and solder the joints on the other side. After soldering, rub all the joints with the wire brush again to remove the excess tallow wax.

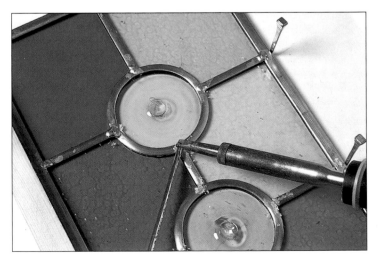

13 Scoop some of the special lead cement out of its container and put it onto the panel. The idea is to fill the gaps between the glass and the lead to weatherproof and strengthen the panel. You can use the spatula end of the fid or a brush to spread and push the cement under the cames.

14 When you have filled all the gaps on one side of the panel, put on the rubber gloves and scatter some of the whiting powder over the panel and spread it with your hand. This powder will help to dry the oily cement and eventually to clean the glass. Turn the panel over and do the other side in the same way. Leave the panel to dry for approximately one hour. Do not leave overnight or the cement will become too hard to remove from the surface of the glass.

15 "Draw" the pointed end of the fid down the sides of the leads, digging through and separating the excess cement from that which remains under the lead cames. Turn the panel over and do the other side.

16 Now start to brush the excess cement off the glass and the lead cames. Brush in all directions but especially across the leads. The cement and whiting will slowly be removed and the panel will start to look cleaner. Keep brushing, concentrating on the leads, and stop occasionally to see where the cement is still clinging to the sides of the lead. Draw the fid down the lead to remove excess cement. Change to a cleaner brush. As you keep brushing, the leads will become darker and the glass cleaner. Leave the panel flat on the table overnight so the cement under the cames can become really dry and firm.

The frame for this table mirror is made with opalescent glass to obscure the shape of the mirror behind, as it would be impossible to cut an angle such as a deep V from mirror glass. Some opalescent glass is too dense to see through when laid on a table, so you will have to make paper or card templates. These are then laid on top of the glass and their outlines marked out with a felt tip pen.

You will need

12 " x 6 " (30 x 15.5 cm) red opalescent glass

6 " x 3 " (15.5 x 7.5 cm) pink opalescent glass

12 " x 12 " (30 x 30 cm) mirror glass, 1⁄16 " (2 mm) thick

scissors

thin felt tip pen

glass cutter

grozer/breaker pliers

carborundum stone

7⁄32 " (5 mm) copper foil

fid

flux brush

flux

soldering iron

approximately 3 sticks of solder

galvanized steel or copper wire

1 Enlarge the template on page 93 to the correct size and make two copies of it. Cut out the shapes for the frame from one of the templates and put the heart shape in the middle to one side. Cut as close to the inside of the pen line as possible to prevent the glass pieces increasing in size when you score them.

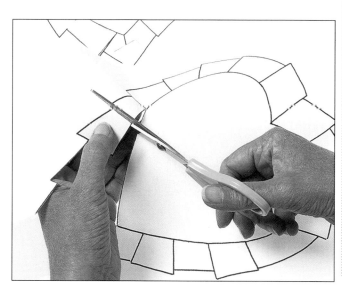

2 Lay the templates individually onto the surface of the glass and mark around each one with a thin felt tip pen. Leave some space between each piece.

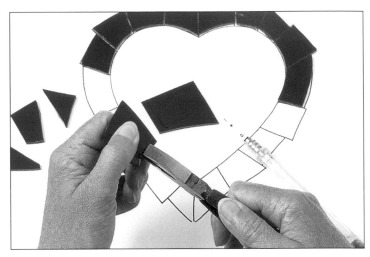

3 Make scores with the cutter along the inside of the felt tip pen lines for each piece. Use pliers to snap out the pieces, holding the pliers close to the score and gripping the glass tightly with the fingers of the other hand. Snap any excess glass from the shape you want.

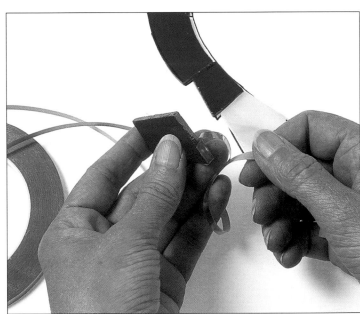

4 Rub the edges of the glass pieces along the carborundum stone to blunt them and to provide a "key" for the foil. Carefully wash and dry all the pieces. Copper foil all pieces and fold the excess down onto the sides of the glass. Rub down with the fid.

artist's tip

When you have both hands full, holding a soldering iron in one hand and glass in the other, and you need to apply solder at the same time, be prepared: curl a length of solder so that it sits upright on the table and melt small amounts from the end of the stick as needed.

5 Arrange the pieces on the spare template. Make sure all the inside edges line up. Apply flux with a brush.

6 Tack solder the pieces together. Apply more flux over all the copper foil and bead solder the seams. Tin solder the sides. Turn the frame over and tin solder the back.

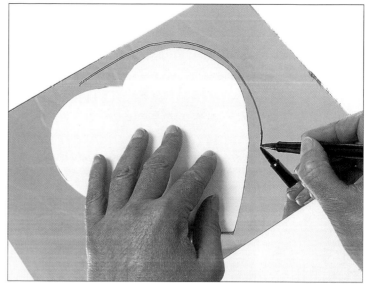

7 Now lift the frame into a vertical position and tin solder the inside and outside edge of the frame. You can use up any blobs of solder that have collected there from soldering the front. If the solder doesn't flow well, apply more flux. Wash the frame carefully in warm soapy water and rinse with clear water.

8 Take the heart shape left from the first template and place it onto the reflective side of the mirror glass. Draw around the shape leaving a margin of about ⅝" (1.5 cm) and drawing a straight or rounded shape at the top where the heart turns into a deep "V". This deep "V"-shape cannot be cut from the mirror. Score and break the mirror. Copper foil, flux and tin solder the edges of the mirror, then wash and rinse.

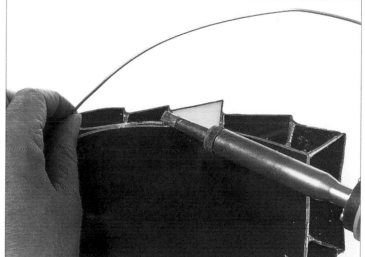

9 Lay the heart frame facedown onto a flat surface and place the mirror, reflective side down, on top of it. Check that the edges of the mirror are hidden behind the frame when viewed from the front. Apply dabs of flux onto the seams of the frame. Melt a small amount of solder so it flows from the edge of the mirror and onto the seams of the frame, joining the two together. Continue around the whole frame.

10 To make the stand, bend the wire as in step 5 on page 31. Solder the bent-up ends along the mirror edge and across the seams of the frame. Once soldered, the stand can be adjusted until you are satisfied with the tilt of the mirror.

Tropical Fish Panel

C opper foil is ideal for assembling small window panels with intricate design elements and small shapes. It is flexible and has a sculptural quality, enabling you to wrap it around the glass with ease. This small window panel could be framed like a picture and hung in front of an existing window, or adapted in size to fit into a cupboard door or a small internal window.

You will need

18 " x 12 " (46 x 30 cm) pale blue water glass

18 " x 12 " (46 x 30 cm) turquoise water glass

12 " x 12 " (30 x 30 cm) rich blue antique or other glass

4 clear medium nuggets

6 " x 8 " (15.5 x 20.5 cm) grey glass

4 " x 6 " (10 x 15.5 cm) clear patterned glass

3 bright yellow small nuggets

6 " x 12 " (15.5 x 30 cm) bright yellow glass

glass cutter

grozer/breaker pliers

carborundum stone

¼ " or ⁷⁄₃₂ " (6 or 5 mm) copper foil

fid

flux brush

flux

soldering iron

solder

rubber gloves

black patina

U.V. glue

1 Enlarge the template on page 94 to the correct size and make another copy. Lay the pieces of colored glass over one template and score all the elements of the window. When scoring the background waves, ignore the small half-circle shapes which will accommodate the glass nuggets: simply follow the line of the wave and score straight through the small circle. It is easier to score and break out this shape separately later on.

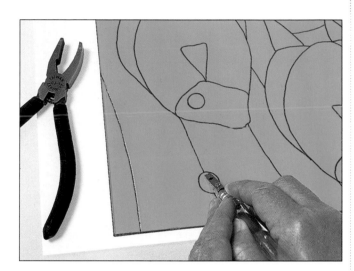

2 Continue the wave score straight through the fish, rejoining the line of the wave on the other side. Cutting small, deep circles and some types of curves from the glass can be awkward. By cutting these later, you will achieve a more accurate result.

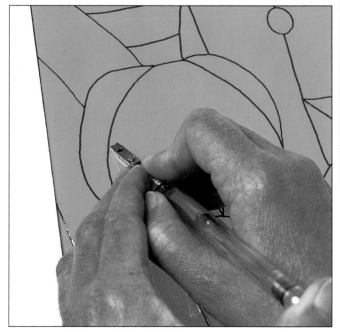

3 Break the long scores first. Note the position of the hands while holding and gripping the glass. Place the glass waves back on the template, and score the half-circle shape and the curve around the top of the fish.

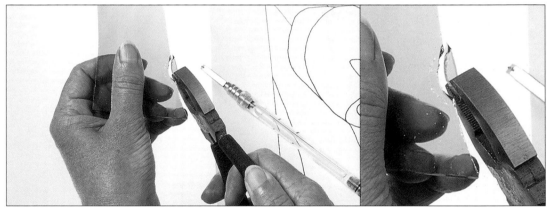

4 Grip the glass with the tip of the pliers and gently but firmly pull it in a downward movement to loosen the score before pulling out the half-circle. Now remove the curved section around the top of the fish.

5 Cut the main body of the fish from the rich blue glass, leaving the deep curve next to the head of the fish to be broken separately. So as not to lose the sharp points around the head, make several smaller scores into this concave shape first. Now hold the glass firmly with one hand and use the pliers to grip and remove the smaller curves, one after the other, until you reach the final score.

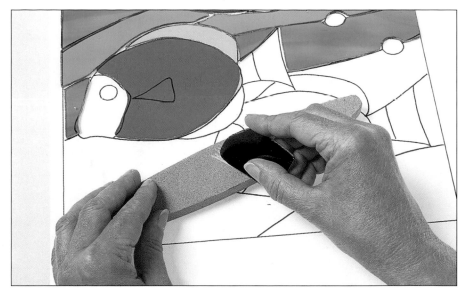

6 When all the pieces have been cut, lay them out on the spare template and check that you are happy with the fit. Rub the edges of all the pieces on the carborundum stone to blunt the glass edges and provide a "key" for the copper foil.

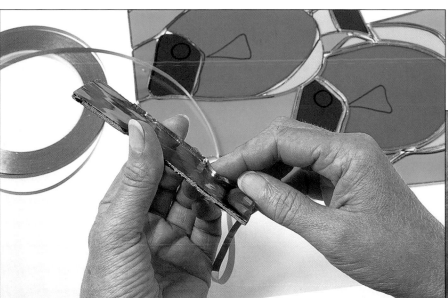

7 Rinse the glass pieces to remove the dust, then dry and begin to copper foil them. Center the edge of the glass on the copper foil and make sure equal amounts of foil protrude on either side.

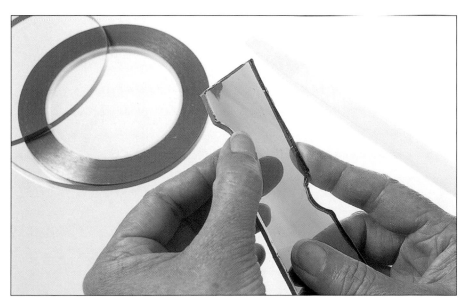

8 Fold the excess foil over onto the sides of the glass with your fingers and make sure the corners are neat.

stained glass/project 12

9 Use a plastic fid to gently rub down the foil so it is completely smooth.

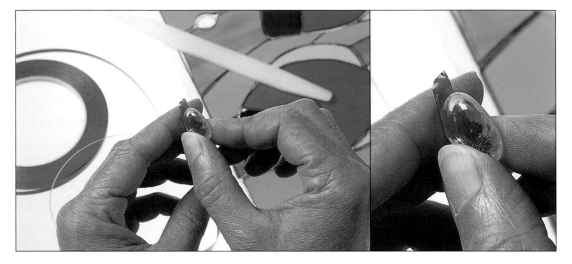

10 Rub the sides of the nuggets on the carborundum stone and wash off the dust. Copper foil and carefully smooth down the wrinkles in the foil with the fid.

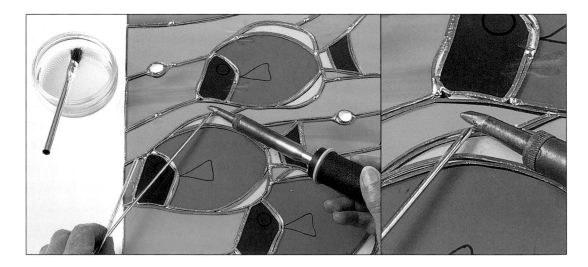

11 Position all the copper foiled pieces on the spare template. Check that all the pieces fit snugly next to one another. Apply dabs of flux to the seams and tack solder the pieces of glass in place.

12 Now apply more flux over all the copper seams and proceed to bead solder. Touch the solder to the tip of the iron from time to time to melt it and move the soldering iron steadily and very slowly along the copper foil seams. Apply just enough solder to form a slightly rounded, smooth seam to cover the joints. Tin solder the front of the panel edges. Once the front is completed, turn the panel over and tin solder the back. Lift the panel into a vertical position and tin solder the edges. Any solder that has collected here from soldering the front can be melted along the edges. Wash the finished panel in warm soapy water and rinse it. Wearing rubber gloves, apply black patina to the soldered seams and the edges. Wash the panel again in warm soapy water to remove the patina solution and rinse with clear water.

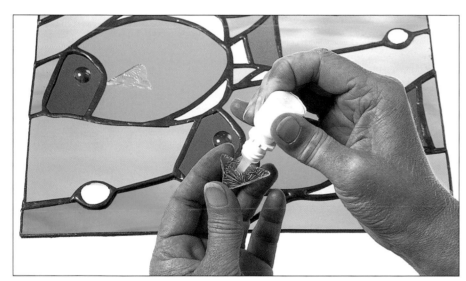

13 Dry the panel and lay it onto the spare pattern. Cut the small textured glass pieces for the fins. Now you can attach the small nuggets for the fish eyes and the fins to the panel. Apply a small amount of U.V. glue to the flat side of the nuggets and the smooth side of the textured glass and carefully position on the glass. Leave to set in a bright room with natural light.

Alternative design:

Fish pendant

Instead of making a whole panel, you can also use the fish shape individually. To make a lightcatcher (or a mobile with several fish), copy the template from page 94, cut out one fish shape and enlarge it to the desired size. Foil all the pieces, bead solder the interior joins and tin solder the back and sides. Apply patina in black or copper if desired, then add a wire loop to the top of the fin for hanging.

Window
Gallery

Tropical fish
Artist: Anna Sklovsky
Anna is primarily a glass artist but also designs textiles and her work in the one medium influences the other. The fish in the panel [above] have been sandblasted with patterns inspired by fabric prints.

Jug of Flowers
Artist: Anna Sklovsky
This window panel commissioned for a private residence was painted in some areas for both detail and shadow. The full bloom of the flowers and warm colors make an uplifting and pleasing display.

Ophelia
Artist: Annette Reed
The studio in which this artist works is a fifteenth-century farmhouse with a crescent-shaped moat. This, and her love of Shakespeare and all things medieval, inspired the theme for this richly colored window. She also experiments with painting on glass to see the different textures and effects she can create.

Fish scales
Artist: Annette Reed
The artist wanted to reproduce an effect she had previously created for a window depicting a mermaid. She decided to use the idea of fish scales to create a bright and beautiful pattern of coordinating color. The lead work is simple in concept with paint used to define the forms of the scales and swirls.

Tea Time
Artist: Anna Sklovsky
The glass in the foreground of this leaded panel is Victorian etched glass, the background is ribbed glass. Details on the teapot, jug, sugar bowl and cups and saucers are sandblasted off flashed glass.

Zippy the fish
Artist: Annette Reed
This jaunty and detailed roundel was created while the artist was in her second year at Swansea College of Art. The task was to create a window using combing lead and paintwork on a maritime theme. The moon placed behind the fishing net lends perspective to the composition.

Madonna and child
Artist: Anji Marfleet
An elegantly designed memorial window made in lead with a variety of differently shaped bevels and clear glass. A large faceted jewel is incorporated at the top of the window. Although this window is made with clear glass, it casts a rainbow of colored light into the room. It was made for the Lady chapel in a Catholic Church in Barnsley. Yorkshire.

The appliqué method of building up a picture in glass can be very rewarding. Colored glass is glued to a base of clear glass and the gaps between the pieces are filled with grout. You may want to fill as much space as possible with pieces of colored glass, or you can leave wider gaps to allow for a bolder, darker outline. The design can be figurative, with the glass cut to specific shapes, or abstract, using pieces of scrap glass almost as you would in a mosaic, or it can be a mixture of both. Small appliqué panels can be framed and hung as pictures.

You will need

8 " x 12 ¾" (20.5 x 32 cm) clear glass, ⅛" (4 mm) thick

8 " x 8 " (20.5 x 20.5 cm) orange or red glass

6 " x 6 " (15.5 x 15.5 cm) bright yellow glass

10 " x 8 " (25 x 20.5 cm) lime green glass

10 " x 8 " (25 x 20.5 cm) medium green glass

10 " x 8 " (25 x 20.5 cm) dark green glass

glass cutter

grozer/breaker pliers

carborundum stone

"wet and dry" sandpaper

small block of wood

felt tip pen

6 small tubes of U.V. glue

plastic bowl

household filler

universal black stainer

rubber gloves

plastic fid or spatula

sponge

cloth

household glass cleaner

1 Enlarge the template on page 92 to the correct size and make three copies. Lay the differently colored glass over one of the templates and score and break the individual shapes and colors, following the template. As you work, lay the cut pieces onto the second template to keep the cutting template clear and tidy. You may find it useful to use two sets of pliers to break the long, narrow shapes of the grass. Place the jaws next to either side of the score and snap the glass apart.

2 Prepare the clear piece of glass by rubbing the edges along the carborundum stone to blunt them. You must be careful not to rub too hard, as this will fracture the edges. Alternatively, you can use a piece of "wet and dry" sandpaper wrapped around a small block of wood and dipped in water to smooth the sharp edges of the glass. Clean the clear glass thoroughly, and place it on top of the third template.

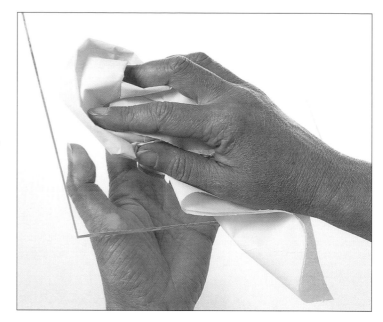

3 Start laying the colored glass pieces onto the clear glass to see how the shapes fit. If any piece is too long, or needs to be trimmed, mark it with a felt-tipped pen and place it back on the table to cut or groze with the pliers. The poppy heads and the long grasses should be glued down first.

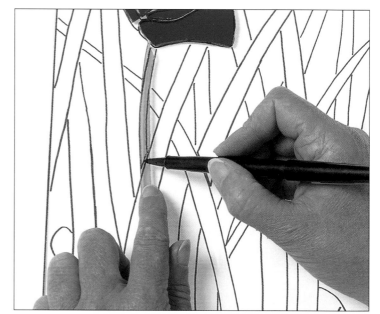

artist's tip

While the U.V. glue is still wet, take care that the glass pieces do not slide around and set before you are able to readjust them.

4 You can leave gaps between the pieces of glass - in this project it is not vital that the pieces lie next to each other perfectly.

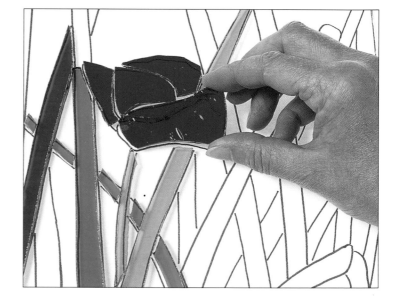

5 Apply glue to the back of each piece, and position it onto the clear glass base. Make sure there is plenty of glue around the sides of each piece: if there are gaps, the grout may seep under the glass. If the glass has become dirty from handling, carefully clean the back with a lint-free cloth before applying the glue. If you are in a room with natural sunlight, the pieces will adhere quite rapidly. If the room is not lit with natural light, the glue takes much longer to set.

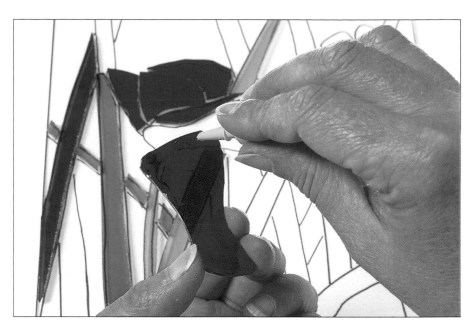

6 Once the poppy heads and long grasses are firmly set, the picture can be built up further by continuing to add more shapes and colors. The glass can be laid directly on top of the panel and shapes marked out with a felt-tipped pen before scoring and breaking. Look at the off-cuts: you may find that some of these are suitable for slotting into the gaps. Be creative with even the smallest pieces, and take time to experiment with various shapes before you commit yourself to gluing them down. The smallest pieces of red, which appear between the blades of grass in the finished panel, were small off-cuts from cutting the larger poppies. Glue down the extra pieces and leave to set.

7 In a plastic bowl, mix the household filler, following the manufacturer's instructions, and some black stainer. Do not make the mixture too wet. Wearing rubber gloves, use a plastic fid or spatula to spread the filler over the panel and fill the gaps between the glass pieces. When you have finished grouting, wipe the excess filler off the surface with a damp sponge. This will also smooth the filling in the gaps. When the glass is clean, leave the filler to dry. Finally, clean the glass with a cloth and remove any smears with household glass cleaner.

Candle Lamp

O palescent glass reflects light and therefore does not depend upon backlighting to reveal its color. Commonly used for lampshades, opalescent glass obscures the light fittings within and, when illuminated, the colors and features of the glass are highlighted. The opacity of opalescent glass can vary. This candle lamp is made with a wispy or semi-opalescent glass.

You will need

18 " x 10 " (46 x 25 cm) of amber wispy or semi-opalescent glass

stiff paper or card

fine felt tip pen

glass cutter

cutting square

grozer/breaker pliers

carborundum stone

¼ " (6 mm) copper foil

fid

flux brush

flux

soldering iron

4 sticks of solder

12 " (30 cm) fine copper wire

snippers

24 " (61 cm) copper wire, approx. 1.5 mm (16 gauge)

round-nosed pliers

tea light

black patina

sponge

rubber gloves

1 Enlarge the template on page 93 and transfer it to stiff paper. Make sure the sides are perfectly straight. Lay the template onto the glass (lining it up against a straight side of the glass if there is one) and draw around it with a fine felt tip pen. Turn the template upside down, butt it up against the line you have already drawn and trace around the template with the felt tip pen. Continue in this way until you have all five pieces marked on the glass.

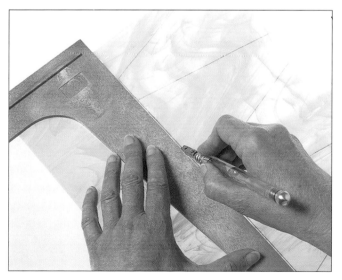

2 Score straight across all the tops and bottoms of the drawn shapes first. Break off the excess glass, then score and break each piece until you have five panels. They must be exactly the same and have perfectly straight sides. File the edges on the carborundum stone, then rinse off the dust and dry. Copper foil each piece and smooth out the foil with the fid.

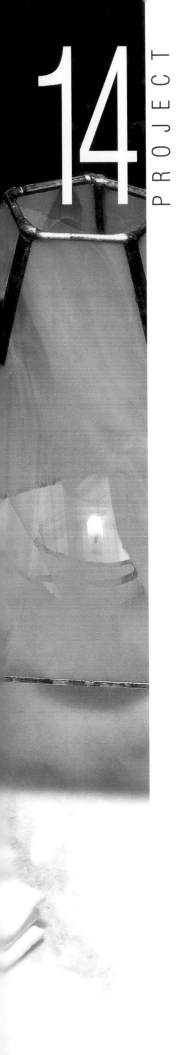

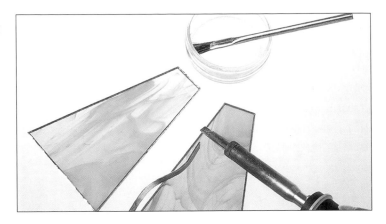

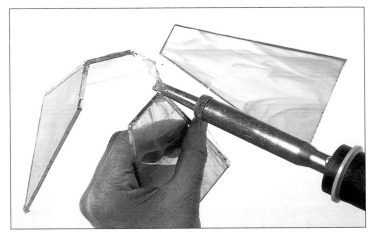

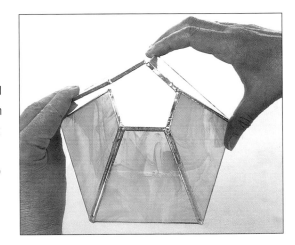

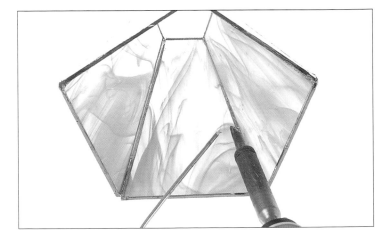

3 Apply flux with a brush and tin solder the front and the back of the pieces, keeping the edges free from bumps.

4 Assembling the lamp requires patience and a steady hand. Place two pieces together at an angle and dot solder onto the top corner joint. Position the third and then the fourth panel, aiming for a pentagon shape at the top. Only dot with solder so that you can remelt and adjust the angles if necessary.

5 Now check carefully that the fifth piece will fit correctly. If it does not, readjust the angles of the other pieces by melting the tiny drops of solder on the corners and repositioning the panels until the fifth piece fits comfortably. Solder it into place, then check all the bottom edges fit snugly together and melt a tiny amount of solder to hold them together at each joint. Melt more solder neatly along and around the top edge of the lamp to give it a smooth finish.

6 Lay the lamp on its side and tin solder the inside seams. The soldering iron can be used at an angle so the corner of the tip can run along the angles of the inside seams.

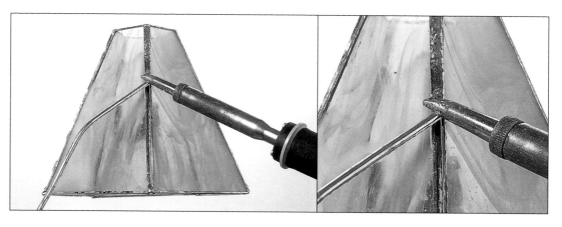

7 Now support the lamp with a piece of wood or other prop so the side seams are in a horizontal position. A shoe box can be useful, with the lamp propped into position with crumpled paper. Once in position, solder along each outside seam to fill any gaps.

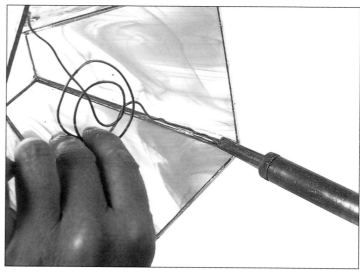

8 For the tea light holder, cut a piece of copper wire about 10 " (25 cm) long. Hold the tea light in one hand and wrap the center part of the wire around it to take the shape. As you wrap around for the second time, tuck the wire underneath and bend it at a right angle to form a loop that will act as a "ledge" for the light to rest on. Leave a length of wire on either side and bend the ends at right angles so they can be soldered to the seams. Manipulate the wire so it lies along opposite seams.

9 Hold one end of the candle cradle onto one inside seam of the lamp and brush some flux onto the part to be soldered. Copper transmits heat quickly so you may need to hold the cradle with pliers. Melt the solder over one end of the copper wire so it becomes secured to the inside seam of the lamp. Do the same on the other side.

10 Measure and snip off five equal lengths of the thicker copper wire. You will need approximately 4 " (10 cm). Curl the ends with some round-nosed pliers. Lay the lamp on its side and solder the legs into the seams. Only solder approximately 1 " (2.5 cm) of the total length into the seams. Once all the legs are soldered into position they can be adjusted so that the lamp sits steadily on the table. Wash the lamp thoroughly in warm soapy water and rinse. Finally, wearing the rubber gloves, apply the black patina with a sponge. Wash gently once again and rinse thoroughly.

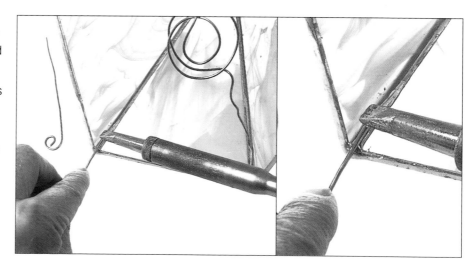

Butterfly Roundel

You don't have to make an entire window to appreciate the effect of stained glass. A small panel or free-form object can hang in a window and be infused with light. This round panel incorporates glass nuggets, small rounded lumps of transparent or opaque glass. They are available in a wide variety of beautiful colors and different sizes. Glass nuggets can be foiled, leaded and even glued, adding character to windows, lamps and three-dimensional pieces of work.

You will need

12 " x 12 " (30 x 30 cm) leaf-green streaky glass

12 " x 12 " (30 x 30 cm) dark green water glass

6 " x 6 " (15.5 x 15.5 cm) red, yellow, amber and grey glass

6 bright yellow glass nuggets

glass cutter
grozer/breaker pliers
black felt tip pen
carborundum stone
7/32 " (5 mm) black-backed copper foil
fid
flux brush
flux
soldering iron
solder
2 " (5 cm) copper wire
rubber gloves
sponge
black patina
strong thread or fishing line

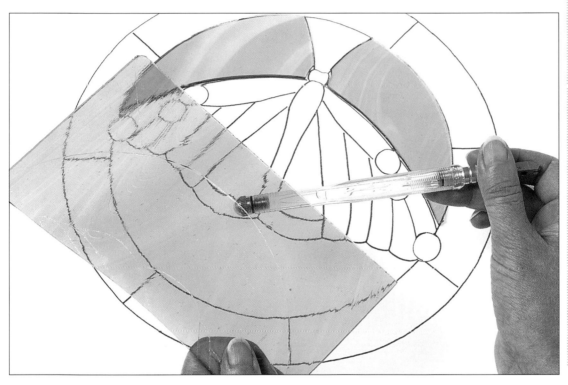

1 Enlarge the template on page 93 to the correct size and make another copy. Using one of the templates, score the background sections first. Tap the score on the underside of the glass to "loosen" the fracture and help ease the pieces out when you use the pliers. Note the series of small curved scores already made on the left side of this piece of glass. These scores are for the shape around the bottom edge of the butterfly. It is sometimes useful to make all the necessary scores first and then lift the glass off the pattern to break off the unwanted pieces.

2 Use the pliers to grip the glass and "pull" out the series of small curves for the bottom edge of the butterfly design. If they stubbornly resist breaking, tap them gently from underneath first to loosen the score.

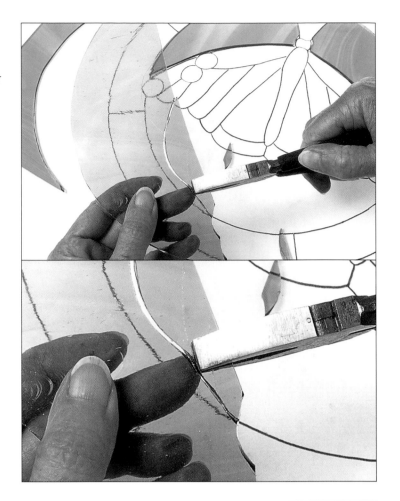

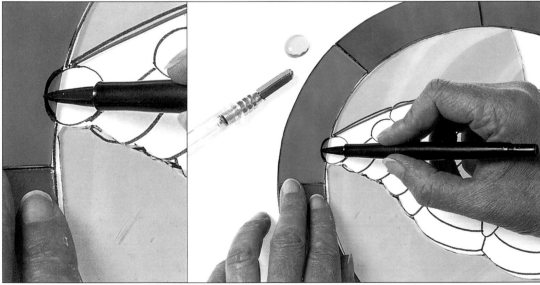

3 Score and break all border segments from the dark green glass ignoring the small curves on the template. Place the border segments on the template and check for a neat fit. Now select a nugget you want to use and place it onto the template and over the green border (remember that glass nuggets vary in size and shape – each one is different). Mark around it with black felt tip pen. You can now score this small half-circle from the green border. To break it, tap the glass from underneath and use the pliers to "pull" it out. Use the same method for the right-hand wing tip.

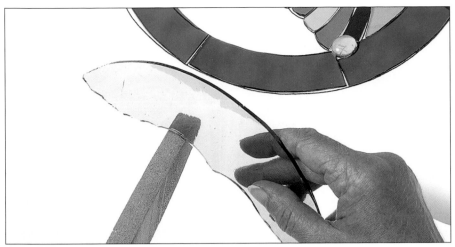

4 Gently rub the edges of all the glass pieces, including the sides of the nuggets, on the carborundum stone to remove any slivers of glass and provide a "key" for the copper foil. Filing the glass also makes it safer to handle.

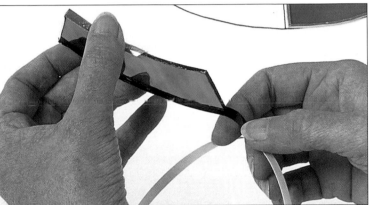

5 Place the edge of each piece of glass centrally onto the copper foil. Apply the foil around the glass edge and overlap the ends where you began. Fold the excess foil down onto the sides of the glass and use a fid to smooth it down onto the sides and the edges. Place the copper foiled pieces onto the spare template and check for a neat fit.

6 Apply dabs of flux with a brush and tack solder the pieces together, melting just a little solder at a time.

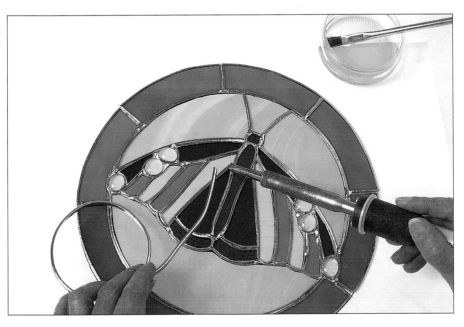

stained glass/project 15

7 Now brush flux along all the seams of the copper foiled glass. The flux helps the solder to flow more easily.

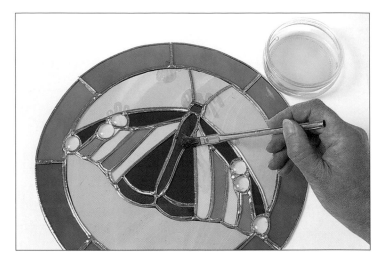

8 By moving the soldering iron very slowly along the seam while touching the tip of the iron with the stick of solder from time to time, the solder should flow to form a "bead", or smooth, slightly rounded seam. Apply enough solder to cover the copper foil and hide the join beneath, but take care not to apply too much. The blobs of solder from tacking can be melted as you work along each seam.

9 Turn the panel over and tin solder the back. Now lift the panel into a vertical position, apply flux all around the edges and tin solder them. You may find there are small bumps of solder that have formed on the edge when you were soldering the front and back. Melt these along the outside edge. Again, don't apply too much solder or it will just dribble down the panel.

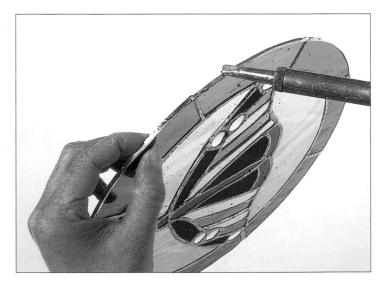

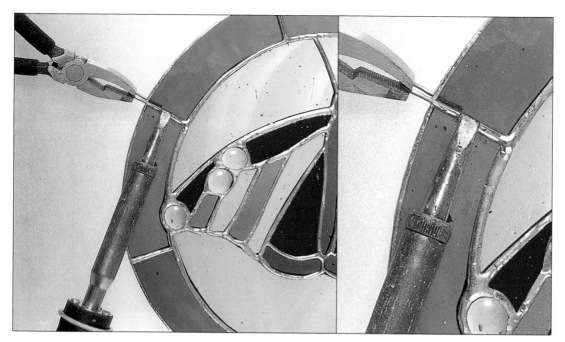

10 Cut two pieces of copper wire to a length of 1 " (2.5 cm) and bend them into two U-shaped loops. Grip one with the pliers and slip it into position so that the wire ends lie along the seam on either side of the panel. Solder one end onto the front, then turn the panel over and solder the other end of the loop onto the back of the panel. Repeat this with the second wire loop. Once the loops are in place, wash the panel thoroughly in warm soapy water, then rinse and dry.

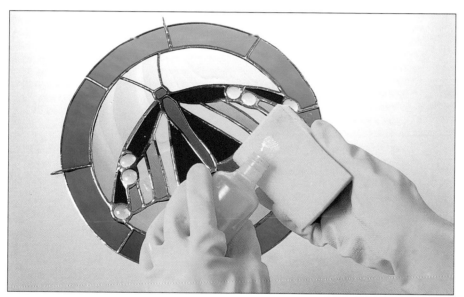

11 To turn the silver color of the solder black, you can apply a patina. Wearing rubber gloves, tip some black patina onto the sponge and gently wipe over all the soldered areas. The solder will take on a grey-black finish instantly.

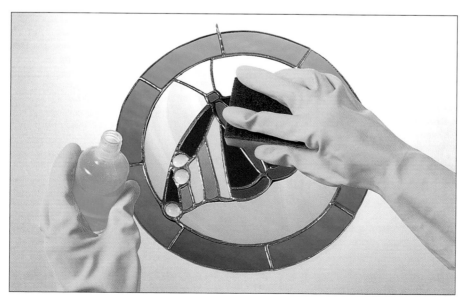

12 Make sure the patina covers all the silver solder, and also apply it to the back and sides. Finally, wash the roundel thoroughly in warm soapy water once again, then rinse. You can hang the roundel in front of a window using strong thread or fishing line.

Templates

All templates must be doubled in size using the most commonly available photocopier zoom size of 141%. First photocopy the required template in the book with the zoom set at 141% enlargement. Then photocopy the copy, also at 141% enlargement. The second copy will be twice the size of the template in the book.

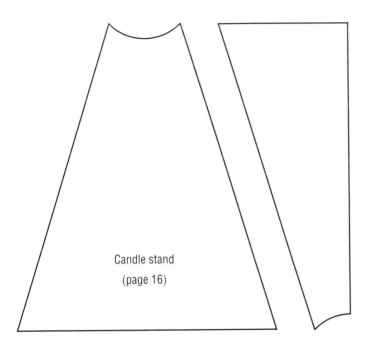

Candle stand
(page 16)

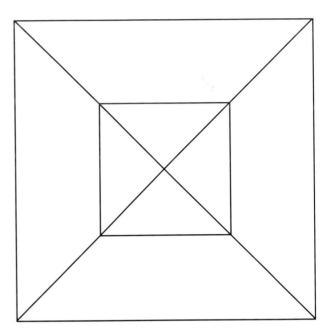

Blue & silver picture frame
(page 28)

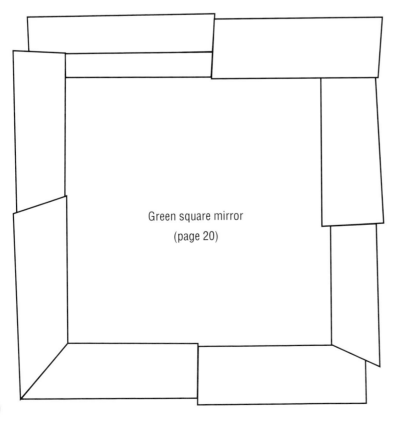

Green square mirror
(page 20)

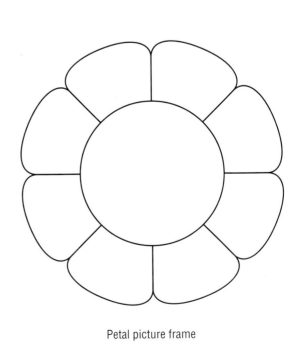

Petal picture frame
(page 46)

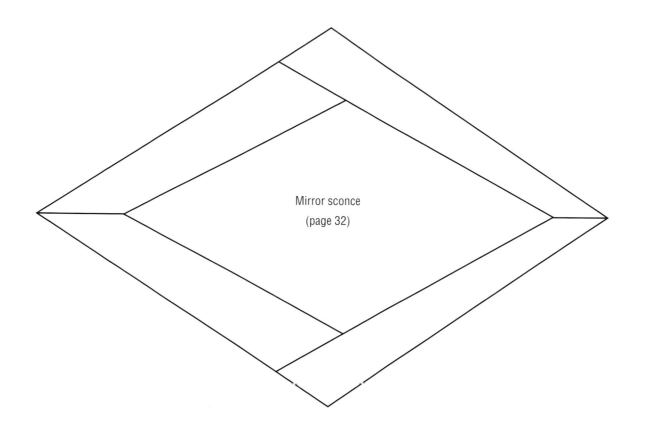

Mirror sconce
(page 32)

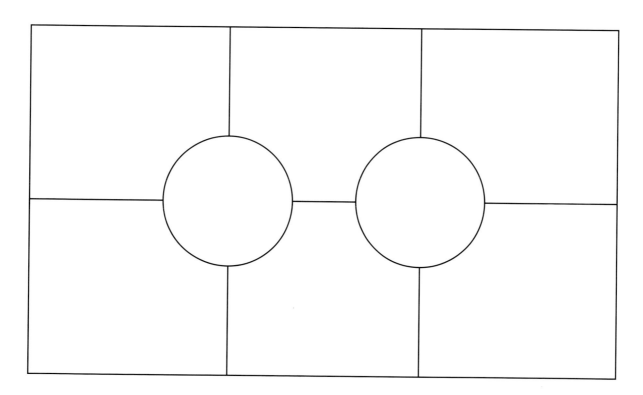

Leaded window panel
(page 58)

side

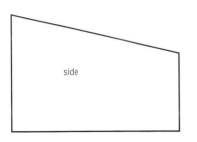

side

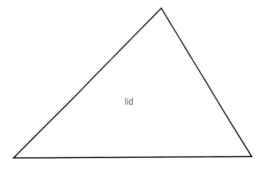

side

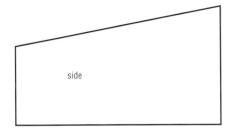

lid

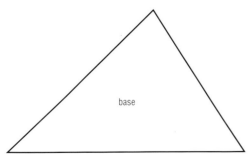

base

Triangular box
(page 36)

Appliqué poppy panel
(page 76)

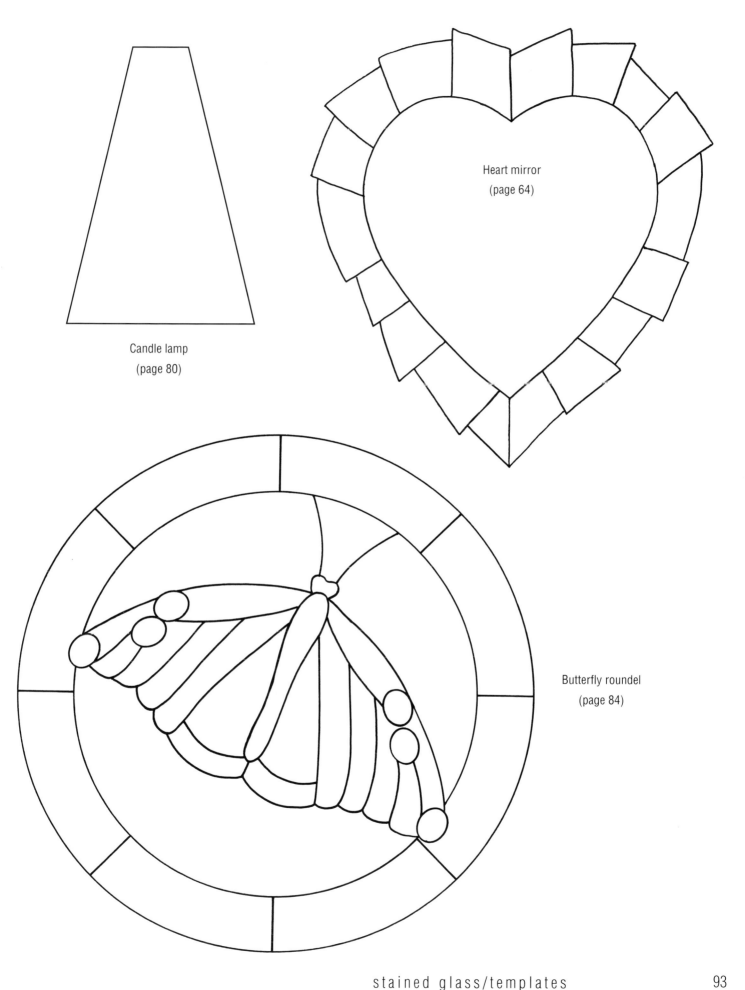

Candle lamp
(page 80)

Heart mirror
(page 64)

Butterfly roundel
(page 84)

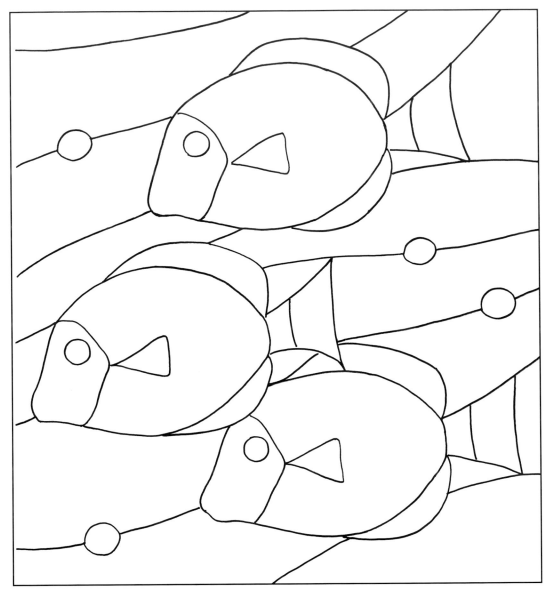

Tropical fish panel

(page 68)

Suppliers

Cathedral Stained Glass
www.cathedralstainedglass.com

Crafts, Etc!
www.craftsetc.com

D&L Stained Glass Supply, Inc.
4939 N. Broadway
Boulder, Colorado 80304
1-800-525-0940
www.dlstainedglass.com

Delphi Stained Glass
1-800-248-2048
www.delphiglass.com

Diamond Tech International
5600-C Airport Blvd.
Tampa, Florida
1-800-937-9593
www.dticrafts.com

Glass Crafters
398 Interstate Court
Sarasota, Florida 34240
1-800-422-4552

Glass Crafts Online
www.craftsfaironline.com

Hobby Lobby Creative Centers
www.hobbylobby.com

Hudson Glass Co., Inc.
219 North Division Street
Peekskill, New York 10566-2700
1-800-431-2964

McGills Glass Warehouse
7121 Radford Avenue
N. Hollywood, California 91605
818-765-1280
www.mcgillsglass.com

Spectrum Glass Company
P.O. Box 646
Woodinville, Washington 98072
425-483-6699
www.spectrumglass.com

Stained Glass Warehouse
8535 Baymeadows Road, Suite 39
Jacksonville, Florida 32256
904-732-4727
www.stainedglasswarehouse.com

Warner-Crivellaro Stained Glass
1855 Weaversville Road
Allentown, Pennsylvania 18103
1-800-523-4242
www.warner-crivellaro.com

Index